isters of the Flame

An Introduction to the Ascended Masters
of the I AM America Teachings

Lori Adaile Toye

I AM AMERICA TRILOGY: BOOK TWO

I AM AMERICA PUBLISHING & DISTRIBUTING
P.O. Box 2511, Payson, Arizona, 85547, USA. (480) 744-6188
www.iamamerica.com

I AM America Maps and Books have been marketed since 1989 by I AM America Seventh Ray Publishing and Distributing, through workshops, conferences, and numerous bookstores in the United States and internationally. If you are interested in obtaining information on available releases please write or call:
I AM America, P.O. Box 2511, Payson, Arizona, 85547, USA. (480) 744-6188, or visit:
www.iamamerica.com

Graphic Design and Typography by Lori Toye
Host and Questions by Sherry Takala
Editing by Elaine Cardall and Betsy Robinson

Love, in service, breathes the breath for all!

Print On Demand Version

9 8 7 6 5 4 3 2 1

Cover Design by Lori Toye, cover illustration information follows:

The *Torch of Wisdom*, analogous to the Ascended Masters' Unfed Flame of Love, Wisdom, and Power, is an essential topic presented in this book. This thousand-year-old symbol is the inspirational icon of the spiritual trailblazer who leads with the cherished fire of inner illumination. To some esoteric scholars this venerated light is the soulful presence of dharma, which gives meaning and purpose to our spiritual journey, and ignites our consciousness to receive guidance at life's important junctures of human growth and evolution. The flame of Spirit is the heart's innate warmth and kindness that we rely on to light the treacherous path as we traverse the dark valleys of self. Through the intentional cultivation of Mercy, Compassion, and Forgiveness our mental and emotional conflicts diffuse, and the lower-self awakens to the individualized presence of God – the I AM. [1]

1. Johnson, Will. "The Torchbearers." The Theosophical Society (Pasadena) British Section. Web. 26 Nov. 2013. <http://www.theosophical.org.uk/newsletter/archived-feature-articles/the-torchbearers/>.

*"A mighty flame followeth
a tiny spark."*

- Dante

Contents

CONTENTS

Introduction

When I was asked to do the structural editing for this trilogy, I was eager to work with the Ascended Master Teachings. I had been a long-time follower of Lori's work, had read all her books, and had a profound respect for her process of receiving information. Most important to me were the Ascended Master Teachings which brought forth a simple plan for peace and prosperity for All and a direct way to align with our I AM Presence. With each of us having a special place of love within Creation and the ability to choose to be an effective part of building a loving world, I wanted to help the Ascended Master Teachings reach as many people as possible.

In the process of preparing Teachings for publication, one word could be missing from a sentence within a transcript, making an entire concept unintelligible. To be able to work with the utmost care and respect, I felt I needed to establish my own working relationship with these Ascended Masters, so I could ask about enigmatic passages. Forming these relationships became an inestimable highlight of my experience with this trilogy. Mostly, they would assist me but sometimes, they would just let me ponder. Their work is layered with meanings, so pondering proved to be a useful process, for much becomes clear this way. There were also times, I felt a phrase or a reference was so far beyond my mental skill that I just let it be, hoping that someone else could put it to good use.

The first part of this trilogy, *A Teacher Appears,* provides a conceptual bridge from our cultural beliefs to the work of the Ascended Masters and the Plan of the Hierarchy for the evolution of ourselves and our planet. There are techniques for healing, manifesting, protection, projecting consciousness, and aligning Chakras. Recognizing the I AM Presence as our Higher Self, we are able to make a quick and easy connection to I AM THAT I AM. Explanations are given about Earth Changes, uses of Color Rays and the Maltese Cross, Universal Laws, and dietary changes. Affirmations are shared that will give us powerful results. The bridge created in this first book is strong enough to take us from fears and limitations into a masterful plan of upliftment and unity.

The second book of the trilogy, *Sisters of the Flame,* brings forth the nurturing side of our being, the female principle, which can recognize the needs of the Earth Mother. The Earth Changes are presented as a reflection of our collective consciousness that activate in order to correct imbalances. Being responsible on an individual level for the energies we hold and radiate, we all create global balance or imbalance. The information on the Earth Changes is designed to unite people, for when we know we are truly ONE, we will work together. Integrating with our Higher Self, the I AM Presence, gives us the free movement necessary to be who we really are and to allow others to be who they are. This will avert cataclysmic Earth Changes. Those who know they are an integral part of lifting the Earth Planet naturally form a network of cooperation. Each act of service diminishes separation and lifts our collective vibration.

Holding the Earth Mother within our hearts expands our awareness of who we are and opens us to the Fourth Dimension, where our individual Earth bodies unite with spirit. When we know the great gifts of the Mother and her desire to be impregnated with spirit, we can also feel the brilliant, spiritual light of her inner sun. As her light is most assuredly moving outward to her surface, we can feel our own brilliant light moving outward as well. Are we not also in her image and likeness?

It is appropriate that *Sisters of the Flame* begins with a presentation of the Angelic Host, a nurturing and protective network which can be called into action by our Higher Self and can even appear to us physically. Learning to work with healing and guiding angels makes it is easier to release the machination of an overworked mind. It may be time to release our minds—which have given us the capability to conceive of the spirit—to that Spirit itself.

A Teacher Appears has an abundance of the Blue Ray of Divine Truth and *Sisters of the Flame* overflows with the Pink Ray of Divine Love. At first, it may seem too simple to believe that Creation flows and expresses upon the Color Rays but one can truly experience healing and abundance using the Green Ray. The Pink Ray of Divine Love and the Blue Ray of Divine Truth coalesce to become the transforming Violet Ray, which brings forth directed purpose. The Gold Ray follows, bringing the synthesis of being and the acceptance of the self in service.

This colorful trilogy has the progression of a thesis, antithesis, and synthesis as truth and love merge into perfection. When we have a Teacher who can see beyond the confines of our illusions and we can hold onto the Flame of Transformation, we can become ONE. We lift through this Flame into the *Fields of Light,* the conclusion of this trilogy.

This trilogy also follows the three Ascension sequences of the Earth Planet, with seventeen Golden City Vortices in each. *A Teacher Appears* relates to the I AM America Map of the United States, all of the Americas, and Greenland. This sets the stage of the I AM Race and the attributes of I AM. *Sisters of the Flame* relates to the Greening Map of China, Asia, Australia, and India and the ecological Alchemy and Oneness with the Earth Mother. The third part of the trilogy, *Fields of Light,* relates to the Map of Exchanges of Europe, Middle East, and Africa. This sequence brings the inner marriage of the male and female aspects, birthing unity consciousness.

What is happening now which makes this the right time for this trilogy? It may be essential, at this time, to embrace a global way of thinking and being. Also, there is a pressing need to know the Plan of the Hierarchy. Trust and understanding may be the best way to accept necessary changes. Many skills are offered by the Ascended Masters to help us meet the challenges we live with today; these skills address our individual and global needs for healing and upliftment. This trilogy—a contemporary guide to the body/spirit and the tasks at hand—is designed to open us to solutions and an ease of living for All. These teachings are not static but evolving. The Ascended Masters have returned to show us the way Home and have an abundant love for all.

The five Vortices of the United States hold the balanced male energies of five Ascended Masters: Sananda (Jesus), Saint Germain, El Morya, Kuthumi, and Serapis Bey. They hold the Father Principle within love, wisdom, and power, just as the Earth Mother and the Lady Masters of Mary, Kuan Yin, and Portia, hold the female principle and exemplify the beauty of our Nature. When we stand back in our lives without judgment, we find in the light of that stance, not only the Circle of the Violet Flame of Mercy and Forgiveness but within that circle, a spiral. This spiral holds the electromagnetic trail of those who have gone before. Extending a hand upward to an Ascended Master and allowing ourselves to merge, we can find our true individualized paths within the ONE.

One night, after a long day on this project, upon closing my eyes, I could see a being coming toward me with great speed and purpose. He had an intense gold outline framing a beautiful mosaic of luminous colors. I could feel myself opening to receive energy from this being, whom I then recognized as Saint Germain. The Pink Ray, edged in Blue, began saturating my being. Gradually these two colors merged into an exquisite Violet, which was rejuvenating. Another night, upon closing my computer, I could feel several Ascended Masters collectively thanking me. I had a fleeting glimpse of their comfort before a fireplace in a grand Lodge. Their good-natured camaraderie was contagious and inviting. One for all and all for ONE!

Sananda and I sometimes sit together in silence. All I need to know and feel is in this silence, where the peace of perfect love is revealed. He told me I could always find him in my heart and I do. When I am with Sananda, I am not in any religious sect or concerned with any definition of who he is. He is not the head of any faction which separates and divides people. He comes as a friend, not wanting to be worshipped. He just wants to be with us again. He tells us that we are here to learn to honor the Mother Principle of the Earth, to care for her and respect her needs, and to know we are ONE. This has been sorely missing in this world, causing a grievous imbalance. Sananda says that the feast is prepared. He asks us to drink from the Cup and sup with him.

The more we focus upon the material of this trilogy, the more we become it. Each read-through lifts us to a new level as we learn to surrender to the truth, love, and power of our natural selves. *A Teacher Appears* clears a way and opens our vision to infinite possibilities. *Sisters of the Flame* joins us together to encircle the Earth with the Golden Ray of synthesis, so that we can all lift as ONE. And *Fields of Light* embraces the Source so fully, we become like a child again, trusting, playing, and laughing. This is the birth and innocence of unity consciousness. Becoming ever aware of the Source holding all things together is part of our evolutionary path.

In *Sisters of the Flame,* we learn that the Earth Planet is a schoolroom of immense importance that will serve as a great light for those wanting to move through the Energy Vibration of Emotion, where the greatest gain in evolution has always come. Upheaval is a time of great learning, attunement, and collective reviewing. Though there are some who have been brought to interfere, to tempt, and to test us, we can learn that all things work together as ONE. We are told that all have been brought to this classroom at this time. No matter our circumstances, there are forces which guide and direct us, speaking within our hearts. They are at our beck and call and can open doors and pathways to create happiness and joy in our lives and in all that we do.

We are going Home in a most extraordinary way, all together, with our very own Earth Mother and her many dimensions. If our friends on the other side start appearing to us, they are not popping out of a grave! They have been actively enjoying all the wonderful things in life, just without the sometimes-tedious care of a third-dimensional body. As we lighten our own bodies, we will, in essence, be raising our vibration to meet them. Then we will fly, as our hearts will be soaring. And perhaps, we will even feel the soft thermal of the *Sisters of the Flame* under our wings.

OM EANDRA
(a special blessing for the Earth Mother),

Elaine Cardall

Elaine Cardall is a study group leader in the Golden City of Malton. She is a vegan, mystic, teacher, healer, and writer of songs, prose, poetry, and plays. She lives off the grid, collecting Power from the sun, Love from the rain water, Wisdom from the wind, and Oneness from the Earth. She gives classes with her books *Angel of Joy*, about healing with the Elements in the tradition of the Essene Gospel of Peace and the *I AM Tarot*, which answers questions, reveals Truths, and stills the ego within a reliable system of Inner Dialoguing.

Foreword

Lori Toye entered my world carrying a flame of insight and an explosive new awareness and awe. I had met my first channeler and was I ever impressed! Channeling the Great White Brotherhood was on the other end of the scale from my Medicine woman/shaman training. Lori's work was very important and I wanted to be a part of it. So when Lori was in a trance, I was there asking most of the questions in this book and taping the answers.

Lori was journeying down a long, intense, complex path, being driven and guided to put out the information she received correctly and accurately. This was at a great expense to her personal life. Each person she met along this path jockeyed her into yet another grid of energies, aiding in her growth. The ever-changing structure of her life enabled her to conduct and convey massive amounts of information. Lori enabled those she contacted to make a leap of acceptance into a New Age.

The Masters that Lori channeled always began with "Dear ones." And now they bring you Dear ones *Sisters of the Flame.* "Sisters" refers to the many spiritual teachers and seekers who crossed Lori's path. Everyone shared their perspective and opened doors; everyone touched the other Sisters with loving encouragement. Please allow Lori and the Masters to touch you, leading you into the depths of your soul in the search for enlightenment. There you can ignite a fire of enthusiasm for life and step into the flame of your own frequency—resonate in joy.

Sherry Takala

Preface

Reader,

Prior to the printing of the I AM America Map, when my then-partner first showed me its four-color proof, I was literally breathless. The depth and shadow of the detailed model and the precision photography displayed a rainbow of light streaming from each of the five Golden Cities. This was the late eighties, and every minute detail and feature of the pastel-hued background was created with artful skill that demonstrated years of trained knowledge, that is, no computers or Photoshop! A month before, I had sold my home—to pay for the map's first press-run—but we still needed funds to start our fledgling publishing endeavor. So as soon as we had the I AM America Maps, we loaded hundreds of them into the back of my small car and off we went on a six-week author's tour through Oregon, California, and Arizona. In just a few short weeks, we gave countless living-room presentations, slept on couches, visited numerous bookstores, and shared the information so beautifully illustrated on the maps with thousands of individuals. We found that each networker (lightworker) we met knew another networker; and then that person knew yet another person or important contact. And everywhere we went, we were received with love, appreciation, and unparalleled support for the work and spiritual message of Earth Change.

However, away from the warm embrace of the world family of lightworkers, relatives and friends fidgeted when we'd share an I AM America Map. Our mention of channeling, Ascended Masters, or the nuance of Prophecy or Spiritual Awakening would provoke their awkward body language. Their doubt and skepticism could not be hidden, and our answers to questions like, "Are you doing this for a living?" evoked an uncomfortable silence. It almost seemed biblical and reminds me of a verse from Luke: "They will be divided, father against son and son against father."

This was the part of my and my partner's spiritual journey together that we had never anticipated. Our sincere desire to share the uplifting and timely message of global healing and change was overshadowed by both intense and subtle pressures. Unfortunately, our relationship and friendship couldn't withstand this, and by the spring of 1990 I found myself alone, questioning whether I could even continue my work for the Ascended Masters. I was living in a small apartment, much too small for any type of business office, and with rolling and mailing maps on a daily basis I hardly had time to organize the channeled material. And if I did channel, who could intelligently monitor the sessions?

No doubt I was a bit deflated and emotionally bruised as I sat at Sherry Takala's kitchen table. Her tarot cards, arranged neatly in front of her, patterned a similar tale. "I can help," she softly hinted and paused her reading. "Yes," she assuredly stated, "I can help." In less than one month, she and her husband helped me relocate I AM America to a small town on the banks of the Snake River—Asotin.

Just blocks from Sherry's home, we found a small bungalow with room enough for the children, a large garden space in the backyard, and a tree house hidden in the thick leaves of a walnut tree. I made a solemn promise to my children that this summer would be attentively theirs. Every morning we packed a picnic and by the afternoon we dug our toes into the white sand beaches that dotted the meandering river at the mouth of Hell's Canyon.

In the long, hot evenings while the crickets sang and the air conditioners hummed, I found my way to Sherry's house where I sat at her kitchen table, usually with a group of women, and I channeled. This almost every-other-night channeling session became routine, and before long one of the women who participated volunteered to tape and transcribe the sessions. Many of these transcribed sessions are contained in this book.

This steady practice and Sherry's constant encouragement transformed my style of trance work. In my beginning days as a clairaudient trance channel, I would often lie down on a couch, similar to the style used by Edgar Cayce, also known as the *Sleeping Prophet*. Sherry thought this method much too antiquated and encouraged me to sit up straight in a chair. I felt a bit self-conscious, but with her unceasing assurance that this was better, I soon became comfortable with the technique and the voices of Saint Germain, Kuthumi, Kuan Yin, and Mary and their indelible spiritual wisdom echoed throughout her home.

Before long, word about the sessions at Sherry's spread throughout the local metaphysical community. Sometimes there would be six or seven women sitting for a session. And if you had the good fortune to call our I AM America office in those early days and Sherry answered, an invitation to visit us in Asotin accompanied your map order. Spiritual seekers came from everywhere posing soul-pressing questions about everything from Tesla energies to spiritual development, along with more intimate queries about relationship or health issues. However, the best material flowed within our original small group of women: Sherry, Lynne, and Glenda—the *Sisters of the Flame*, affectionately coined by Master Saint Germain.

Prior to one session, a skeptical participant once asked, "How do you know that what you are receiving is from the light?" Ignoring the subtle stab, Sherry protectively asserted, "Why don't you ask for yourself?" The result was a lesson from Saint Germain focused upon the principle of our free will and the individualized Christ Light.

Although I knew the question had been fear-based, I took it seriously and decided that a little extra fortification wouldn't hurt. So when I arrived for the next session I was armed with Alice Bailey's *Great Invocation*. Surely these simple words of love and Brotherhood could light a dark cavern of evil. Afterwards Sherry smirked. "Well, are we going to be saying that every time now?" she asked. Sherry was a practical Medicine woman—a shaman. She knew the difference between dark and light, and if darkness appeared, no doubt, she'd deal with it. So would the Masters.

It was mid-summer and I was biking on the trail along the river about two miles from Asotin, pedaling as fast as I could to outrun an ominous thunderstorm rolling in from the South. Lightning flashed and reflected on the water. Thunder resounded and then the conscious voice of Master Kuthumi spoke to me: "Great Light of Divine Wisdom, stream forth to my being and through your right use let me serve mankind and the planet . . ." Requesting that he please hold that thought, I rushed home with the wind pelting me with large raindrops, and as soon as I got inside, penned several more verses, then went to bed only to be awakened late that night by Saint Germain—with what are now the final words of the *Awakening Prayer*. This prayer, a request and affirmation for worldwide Spiritual Awakening, has been offered in our conferences, our spiritual gatherings, and before channelings. It is printed on the Freedom Star World Map and is published in all of our books. You'll find the prayer in the glossary at the end of this book.

The name of the town where I lived at the beginning of this book—Asotin—is a Nez Perce phrase which means *place of eels*; the indigenous *Nee-Mee-Poo* gathered at Asotin Creek and feasted on eels in the wintertime. A winter camp is a place for rest and dreams, and the heavenly realms feed the needs of the tribe's rich spirituality. Eel is feminine and metaphorically presents emotional challenge that is overcome through clear, decisive thoughts; difficulty is overcome through developing and practicing persistence. No surprise that this same theme is the feminine underbelly of *Sisters of the Flame*.

My time near the dreamy, feminine waters of Asotin was too short, and after one time-compacted year I moved yet again. What remains of my journey are these remarkable lessons from compassionate Master Teachers who, in their multitude of human lifetimes once felt the human ache of loss, and the inequity of swift, merciless change. These teachings recognize the eternal beauty of our hearts and offer the hope and light that shines beyond illusion into the ONE.

As I moved on from Asotin, the spiritual clarity of the Ascended Masters helped me to overcome what seemed like lifetimes of emotional pain during a "Divinely Appointed" crossroads—it was a turning point in my life. Today I know that I ably crossed this junction because of my timely friendship with both remarkable women and Spiritual Mentors. Our loving arms, physical and ethereal, were always ready to hold each other up with every step. Marianne Williamson says, "A friend is willing to take a stand for you . . . even when sitting something out would be easier." Perhaps Saint Germain says this even more simply: "What is love without love? What is love without wisdom?"

Thank you, Dear ones, *Sisters of the Flame*. I AM eternally grateful,

Lori Toye

1

*Angels help us to redefine our spiritual path and assist
the integration process with our Higher Self—the I AM.*

The Angelic Host
Saint Germain

After a long, winding drive down the panhandle of Idaho, I arrive on the white sandy banks of the Snake River in Washington State in the little town of Asotin—situated on the Idaho-Washington border. I pull up to Sherry's home, an older two story home, a bit tattered with a large set of elk antlers adorning the front door and fresh-faced summer flowers newly planted along the walkway. I knock and Sherry answers with a pensive grin on her face. "Okay, tell me everything about the break-up." She pours me a cup of instant coffee, grabs her tarot deck, and we sit at her kitchen table. At this point I'm beyond tears and a bit disheveled. "I'm uncertain just what I should do next," I nervously explain. "The kids are coming for the summer, I know I don't want to stay in Coeur d'Alene, and I have a new tour with the Map in just a week. I'm overwhelmed . . ."

Before I can say anything else, Sherry has laid out the cards, and she flips over the first one. "Well, help is on the way. And you must not stop now . . . you doubt yourself. But they . . ." and she pauses for a minute and points her index finger upward, "They have chosen you to do this."

A dozen questions enter my mind as she flips over each card, yet I can barely form the words to ask.

"You should not worry about money either," she continues. "That is all taken care of . . . see?" And Sherry holds up the Six of Pentacles card, "But you must share your work and what you've been given to do. This is a sacred task you've been entrusted with, and they are always with you."

I was literally mesmerized. Each card held a new story for me—a story beyond my break-up with Dan, a story beyond financial struggle and worry, a story of hope.

After dinner Sherry asked, "Well, will you channel for me?" I was surprised. Not only was Sherry a seasoned psychic, she was also an experienced shaman. My eyes glanced around the room filled with drying herbs and animal skins, and I honestly couldn't imagine that she would hear anything she didn't already know. Yet, here was this wise woman, an elder—for lack of better words—wanting me to trance for her. The words of her tarot reading reverberated in my mind: this is a sacred task.

"Okay, but do you know how to operate a hand-held tape-recorder?"

The lesson that was given that first evening with Sherry is about Angels, and how the Angelic Host links our individual human life force to the Earth. Angels' spiritual help and guidance can instantly change the direction of our life or gently nudge us on the right course of action. They accomplish this through working with our spiritual consciousness—through the influence of the Higher Self, and this is the concept of the Guardian Angel.

After the session, I could tell that Sherry was deeply moved.

"I can help," she gently affirmed. "I can help you find a place to live here in Asotin. And I will work as your assistant until you get back on your feet."

Yes, I definitely have a Guardian Angel! Her earthly name is Sherry.

There are seven classifications of angels of the Angelic Host, each working with their Ray at a particular given moment, each with a directive force and purpose behind their work. The Angelic Host is linked to man [a person], forming a cosmic web to link their life force with that of the primal life force of the Earth Planet. You see, Dear ones, your planet is unique. Long ago, it was determined that this would be a planet where the Angelic Host would be of service to those in physical embodiment. You are indeed so fortunate to have this, for there are planets on which you would embody where they are not allowed to be of service. So, as you seek physical embodiment in this planetary realm, beyond the web of the Higher Self is the web of the Angelic Host.

In particular, each person has seven angels which serve them. There has been much confusion over the Angelic Host as being that of the guides, the guides you speak of in this transitional age. There are those who have gone through previous embodiment with you and impress upon your conscious behavior that which would direct and lead you. There are of the Angelic Host, those who protect and guide you as well. Each of them corresponds to the energy points in your system itself, that which you call the Chakra System and that which we call the Galactic Web. Through the Galactic Web is the cloak of the Angelic Host, here for your protection.

As we look at each of these seven angels, you must understand that they too have their hierarchal purpose. That is not to say, that one is lesser or more than the other but some can function easier in denser areas than others. And so, Dear ones, as we start to look at the Galactic Web and understand the hierarchal angelic force, you will see the vast benefit of becoming aware of their influence in your life, for there are times when they temporarily take on what you would call a physical body to interact with you and direct you. Perhaps you have been at a book store and one will come to you and place a book in your hand or one will gently nudge it off the shelf and it falls to the floor. Have you not had these experiences throughout your life? Things that have turned your life path in a different direction are part of a gentle current which nudges you into the path which you need to be walking.

You may call for their assistance and to increase your awareness is of great benefit to you, for you have seven that have been assigned to you. They work within the realm of Universal Principle and Cosmic Oneness. Some use the concept of split consciousness and others use that of more directive consciousness. Each person has at least one angel who is of a directive consciousness. Many of you have embodied with one of the seven who use split consciousness. The combinations vary. You may have three to four which are split consciousness and the balance with those of directive force. You have seen them at work. You will see a bright light at the corner of your eye or you may sense movement. Their work is closely tied to that of the Elemental Life Forces and you have four angels which work with the four elements.

So, let's look at this in a comprehensive way. As you come into embodiment, you are given one angel which corresponds to one of the points of the Galactic Web. And this is what has been called the Guardian Angel. Some have confused this with the Higher Self. This is inaccurate, for the Higher Self and the one angel of directive force work hand in hand comprehensively. For you see, that of the angelic has the ability to break the layers and density of the physical but only with permission of the Higher Self. It is through your call to the Higher Self that you become more integrated with the Higher Self, but the Higher Self has at its beck and call the directive-force angel.

Now, as you come to understand this concept, I would like to explain to you the six other angelic forces. Whereas, some have perhaps just one directive force angel, there are some that have up to six. It is no mistake that there are those who embody and are very charismatic. The Angelic Host has come and penetrated levels of physical density to aid, and directs each life. How is this so? Through cooperative work with the Higher Self.

Each human being, each soul entity seeking physical embodiment, penetrates the layers of density into physical embodiment, and comes with four angels who correspond to the elements. You have air, fire, earth, and water. And no, they are not Elemental in life force but their directive resonance is that corresponding to Elemental Force. There are some instances where your directive angel is of the water nature or your directive angel is of the fire, or air, or earth. Each of you holds the Divine Blueprint which is yours individually. And while none of you have been given less or more, there are just those of you who utilize more of what you've been given. Now, I hope I have given a clear outline of this information and will open it up for a period of questions.

Question: "You said that the angels are working with our energy systems, are they aligning us as we sleep?"

They work with you in waking and sleeping hours. Those you term the guides, come to you much more in the sleeping hours. The Angelic Host has been able to penetrate both dimensions. Let us take this one step further. There are those who realign the body and keep the physical body functioning, which you understand as healing. Remember again, they work with the ONE God Source and they work in cooperation with the Higher Self, for the Higher Self gives them permission to go and complete the work.

There is much confusion, in your age, over the structure of the heavens. And in the truest sense, yes, all come from the ONE true God Source. You have Guides, you have Angels, you have Devas, and you have Elementals. There is so much for you to sort through in this age. And you say: "Yes, we are bringing the memory back of that which we once understood." But now, you seek a level of understanding which is more complete, for the memory was taken so that you could act out the parts and have the experiences. So that now, the memory is rekindled. You really truly know the meaning of which we speak, for you have experienced it. There was a time when you understood these structures but you had not the opportunity to experience their use.

Question: "It just astounds me that there is so much help, so how could mankind be in such bad shape?"

Yes, it has been astonishing to us as well. But we feel compelled to continue to give the information to you. Remember, the key to understanding the Angelic Host is the Higher Self; for again, freewill and free choice is not invaded. It is your call to the Higher Self which allows the Angelic Host to come within your world. There have been times with every individual embodied, where they do ask. Those who work within the Christian organization, as it is called, who seek through prayer and meditation and have no knowledge of the Higher Self, make their calls to Beloved Ascended Master Jesus. They may make calls to these beings and have many experiences of the use of the Angelic Host. How is this available to them? Their call has been heard by the Higher Self, who works in cooperation with the ONE directive force and a directive-force angel is then impressed consciously and activates the other six.

Question: "So the I AM Presence, or Higher Self, does not have the ability to break through the physical layers and that is why they work with the directive-force angels?

This is correct. The Higher Self, as you understand it, is the storehouse of all the good works that man has completed upon the face of the planet. The Higher Self functions as "the treasures stored up in heaven" in Biblical Prophecy. For the Higher Self to penetrate the physical would break Hierarchal Law.

But the challenge is for you to be responsible with the energies you've sent out through the ages and to remember the Source of all that is truly good, all that is truly ONE in the force of united love, the Higher Self. Its activity functions, in what you have come to realize as the inner level, which we understand is another level. And now, we bring the understanding of the Angelic Host and their work, for with the permission of the Higher Self, they do indeed break physical barriers. They have understood the interaction of Elemental Life Force. And while they have always been available to do this work, man has not sought knowledge of their work. Mankind has a tendency, when something is performed which is miraculous in nature, to take the credit. And where is the credit truly due? Of course, the God Source, from the God Source to the Higher Self, from the Higher Self to directive Angelic Host.

And so, the Galactic Web continues to be woven. Those who have worked more comprehensively together share directive-angelic force, which participates via split consciousness. That is why you see groups of people working more comprehensively and cooperatively together. Those who form the different churches and, believe you me, there are many - what is this but shared split consciousness? These people may perhaps all share a point of the Galactic Web, one of the fourth, or of the third, or of the second, or of the first point, and they seek unification on the Web. They feel directed and compelled to work together. "Like minds attract like minds." Now truly, there are no two minds which are precisely the same, for each is an individual. But an aspect is very similar.

Question: "Is it because of the sense of separation that mankind seems to prefer to work in groups or like minds?"

Indeed, it is through the group that the sense of separation is dissolved. But this has also created war due to the human element of always taking the credit. The organization of churches was intended to be for the upliftment of humanity. But those who come together, understanding the aspects which they share, now focus on the aspects which differ. There are those who come together and share the beautiful aspect of the second force. Perhaps they are all sharing the split consciousness of the Beloved Archangel and should they not delight in the fact that they have been united for this one thing to do together? But what happens is they focus on that which is different instead of focusing on that which is the same. Does this answer your question?

Response: "Yes."

There is much to ponder in understanding this and we have only given you a brief outline; however, we felt it was important that you understand. We will be giving you more instructions in calling to this Host for your aid and benefit and work upon the planet. Again, I instruct you in the use of the Violet Flame. And remember, THE LIGHT OF GOD NEVER FAILS. I AM your coworker and friend.

2

Let go of spirit-hampering thoughts, beliefs, and ideas.
The first goal is to think with your heart—this readies
your consciousness for the I AM.

The Mental Plane
Saint Germain

I awoke to birds singing and the brilliant sunlight streaming through the soft curtains in Sherry's guest room. "We've crafted a plan," Sherry announced as we sat at the breakfast table. "I know where there is a new rental a few blocks from here, and once you're approved, Steve and I will move you in with the pick-up. I can store the Maps in my studio and mail them out for you . . . plus, we can record the sessions here in my house and I know someone who can transcribe for you."

I felt the weight of stress lift as Sherry and I drove over to inspect my possible new home. It was an old bungalow with three closet-sized bedrooms and an ancient claw-foot bathtub. It was one the shabbiest homes I'd ever seen, but with my new-found excitement and an unusual sense of buoyant freedom—well, it seemed like a palace! I stood on the front porch and visualized the violet and gold pansies I would plant next to the massive sycamore tree.

When I filled out the application, I hesitated on "job description." Writer? Not exactly—not yet. What if I told the truth: clairaudient trance channel? No way in hell . . . I'd never be approved. Finally I came up with "workshop leader." It sounded halfway acceptable, and it helped that an old acquaintance from the farm town I grew up in worked at the realtor office as a sales associate. Maybe she'll put in a good word for me.

I drove back to my old home in Coeur d'Alene to find my answering machine filled with messages: an order for a dozen maps from Hawaii, and, to my surprise, several messages from both of Dan's sisters and one from his ex-wife, Jane. How odd. Both of Dan's sisters had clearly voiced their negative sentiments regarding me and my spiritual work and there would be no reason for them to call. I'd call Jane.

She sounded scared. "I don't know how to put this into words, but it is apparent that Dan has totally lost it."

"Is he okay?" I asked.

"He's fine . . . but he's not," she answered. "He's written a will, given me a copy and one to his sister Jody, and the reason we've all called, well . . ." She hesitated. "Do you have anything to do with this?"

"I don't know what's going on," I replied, feeling defensive. My palm was sweaty gripping the telephone, so I wiped it on my dress. Dan wasn't the type to engage in any type of long-term planning and now he'd written a will?

"And he's left with Carrie to camp on some mountain, and some channel that they're working with told them they will be taken up in a spaceship. So they're waiting for the Ashtar Command to pick them up!"

I started to giggle but caught myself. Oh god, she was serious.

Spiritual development and growth is the metaphoric razor's edge. At one level, the razor is sharp and precise, and this training can sever years of karmic residue from one's psychology. Yet, this incisive process can create searing emotional pain, and when one is caught up in this swirling dervish of yet-to-be-healed thoughts and feelings, well, almost anything can happen. This is why seasoned gurus, spirit guides, and elevated spiritual teachers are needed. They've been there, done that, and their experience helps students to navigate the unseen spiritual states of consciousness which we must travel through in order to find the true self; wise teachers help keep us in touch with earthly, grounded realities. Apparently Dan had lost touch.

After ending the conversation with Jane, I called my friend Paul. Paul had been involved with self-development for years, and his life's path had not been easy. As a young teenager, he'd arrived home after school to find his father's body—a nightmarish suicide scene. This drove him into insatiable materialism and he mindlessly scaled a corporate ladder of hollow accomplishment. His spiritual void was later filled with EST and Landmark Training that inevitably led him to the Native American teachings of a shaman. Then Paul spent years in wooded mountains, living off of the land and empowering himself through survival skills and vision quests. Perhaps he could offer a sensible answer.

Paul was quiet and patient as I described the conversation with Jane about Dan's condition. He thoughtfully replied, "The result will have two possible outcomes, but either way, Dan will be a great teacher. Perhaps he will fly off, and this will be a miracle—a miracle of faith. Or, he won't. And this will be a teaching about discrimination."

Two days later I received the call I'd been waiting for. I was approved for the rental home and I would soon be living in the warm river valley in Asotin. I would leave the cold, northern lands of Idaho, and hopefully, too, the harsh lessons of loneliness and isolation. As I drove my car, following behind Steve's pick-up truck and the U-Haul loaded with all of my worldly possessions, I couldn't help but smile as we approached the Lewiston Hill and made our descent into the Lewis-Clark Valley. Sunlight and warmth streamed through the windshield of my car, and the sun's golden rays lifted my spirit. "Now my life will change," I murmured, ". . . again." I had no fear, only light and hope.

Several days after unloading boxes and orienting to my new surroundings, I took a break and walked over to Sherry's house. Sherry and her best friend Lynne sat at the kitchen table and Sherry offered me the usual cup of coffee. She'd been busy setting up the new I AM America office; we'd had little time for personal conversation; and I hadn't told her about Dan. As I recounted the story, I could tell they were amused and after a moment of silence, the two howled. "What a great story for National Enquirer," joked Sherry. "He's a bit unhinged."

Sadly, Ashtar Command never arrived for Dan—at least in the physical dimension—and this fact presented a raw, sober look at the whole channeling phenomenon. Was it real or was it merely one person exploiting another's vulnerable mental landscape?

Sherry shook her head, "He really thought he was going for a ride on a UFO?"

So we decided to ask about this in a session with the Spiritual Teachers. Here, we ask Saint Germain, who is the Ascended Master form of Ashtar, why and how we get caught up in thought-forms and hampering beliefs. What follows is a lesson about how spiritual growth challenges our closely held ideas, thoughts, and beliefs. The Spiritual Teachers identify this intellectual terrain of the human experience as the Mental Plane. Spiritual evolution requires a recalibration of the mind, and one begins to make decisions and choices with the heart. This is the beginning of contact with the I AM Presence, and the experience readies the Christ Consciousness within.

⁓

Welcome, Sisters of the Flame. I AM Saint Germain. I have come to you this evening to present a discourse on the Earth and transitional events. I have listened and heard the questions you have prepared and am willing to answer them and shed the light of the Spiritual Hierarchy upon that which you ask. For you see, my

Dear ones, during this Time of Transition, there is much knowledge and much information that is being given to the Earth Plane. There is much to sift through and much to discern. We understand your searching for the truth, the eternal truths. We are always happy to shed our light of truth upon you at this time and give to you that which you seek, for it has been said, "Seek and you shall find, knock upon the door and it is opened." I will assist you in opening these doors and I also ask that you ask, for you see that we are not allowed to infringe upon the freewill. We need your cloak of permission for us to enter and give you the information you seek. Do we have this, Dear ones?

Question: "Yes. Are there different families in the world and in the etheric? Do some of us belong to one family or another?"

There is only one true family and it is of Spirit, that which is ONE within the Christ Light. However, there are those who discern within the gene pool, those that come from the Council of Twelve. And there are indeed twelve which exist on the Earth Plane at this time, twelve specific gene pools. And you have perceived the gathering of the twelve, each going alone to itself. However, they all originate from the ONE Source, that which has embodied as ONE Source upon the planet Terra, or Earth, as you have known it to be called.

Question: "Tell us about Ashtar. Is Ashtar an alien or are they just thought-forms?"

You're talking about a collective force which functions upon a mental plane. It is also closely associated to the Astral realm. However, its function is performed within the mind of man. Do you understand?

Question: 'I think you're saying that because men need to believe this, they've created these thought-forms appearing in a form that they need to see?"

This is precise. I would like to speak to you about the Ashtar entity at this time. Found within the collective pool, what you would know as the mental realm, man has sought to form an analysis of the many questions and answers. Perhaps a person would like to perceive a flower and so they paint a picture of a flower. They visualize the scent of such, the color of such, the form of such, known to what they have seen as the flower. So it is for a person who perceived a God-like being, separated and away from himself, with magical and mystical qualities. We have been viewed as magical and mystical but we assure you, my Dear ones, we are not. We operate from a realm of consciousness which you may tap into and become ONE with, because you are one with the Source. Do you understand?

Response: "Yes."

In the analysis of the mental plane, much harm is done to man. Here, he must learn to pierce above the mental realm, to go beyond thought and thinking, giving up the mind and letting go of rational analysis. For you see, it creates a thought-form, as you have perceived, with a life of its own, found not in Spirit but formed of human thought. For what is the source of mental perception? The human. Do you understand?

Question: "Is that how the Christ Consciousness was formed, or Jesus in his life?"

The Christ Consciousness was formed of the collective unit of spirit, which is now embedded in the hearts of man. For you see, as the entity that you have known as Jesus, the Christ in his incarnation upon the Earth Plane, embodied that of the highest principles of Divine Spirit coming to human form. This human form, which embodied a Christ Spirit, would be perceived as rather dichotomous - a human form that could contain and embody a Spirit so pure and so clean. However, we would like for you to understand that even in embodiment, there was the human factor involved, as there always is, as the flesh is contained.

To specifically address your question of the Ashtar entity or this being which you have spoken about, we would like to give a warning to you about the danger of the mental and the blockage that can occur to keep you away from the ground of pure spirit.

Question: "The danger of Ashtar is that we get caught up in believing what we want to believe; is that what you're saying?"

This is precise. For you see, the mental plane, the mind, has been given for man to function, to collectively understand the element of spirit. However, as man has developed this mental plane, he must learn to let it go, for it was a tool used to plant the garden and the garden is well seeded at this time. It is time to let go of this function that we call the mind and allow entry into the world of collective Spirit - that which we term the universal.

Response: "I'd like to ask some questions about the Earth Changes now."

We are delighted to serve.

Question: "One of the things that I'm quite confused about: at the Time of the Earth Changes, will everyone be lifted off the Earth or will only some be lifted off?"

You see Dear one, when one enters into the Earth Plane, they sign the agreement to stay in human form for a specified period of time. However, you've had the interacting of the human self and the many doors that open. You may sign the agreement to enter the Earth Plane for a period ten years or ninety years, as you perceive in time; however, it is the series of *experiences* that you have agreed to experience. When you have completed the series of experiences, then it is time for you to move on to the realm of spirit, as we call it. You have come here with one function, that is the raising of the body. This is not done in any majestic or magical way. It is done through a series of events, or experiencing a series of events. You perceive these as lessons to move through, to gain in your collective consciousness, that which will assist you in greater service to others.

Question: "Then during the Earth Changes, we may or may not be here, according to the way we live now with our life experiences?"

Yes. Each contains within himself a Divine Blueprint, a Divine Plan. However, you make the choice. For you see, we speak about freewill. You have the choice to stay after a number of experiences or you have the choice to go and receive your enlightenment in other realms of consciousness, as we have shown to you.

Question: "During the actual cleansing of the Earth, will the Earth be void of humans?"

This is not so, for would we create such a wondrous schoolroom, to take our students from it?

Response: "Sounds like we are actually learning during this transition."

It is the purpose for the schoolroom and the events which are to come. Do you see the great benefit of being in human form during this time? What would it serve for you to be removed during this time, which has been predestined through the ages? This is a time of great growth, a time of great learning. It is a critical moment, as a Time of Great Testing and a time of new lessons. Would this be the time that the pupil would be removed from the schoolroom? This is the time that we all sit as students, pupils, and guests, ready to take the test. Ready to be attuned, as you would say, not only to the teacher and not only to what you perceive as time, but to be one who is collectively reviewing.

Question: "Then, that is why the aliens are here. Is it also to learn at this time?"

There are also those who have been brought to interfere. As you have viewed in a test, is there not always a moment that you would like to cheat, that you would perceive a way to find an easier way to take this test?

Question: "Who are those that are here to cheat? Who are they?"

I would like to explain in greater detail, so you gain a greater grasp of this which I have presented to you. Do you not see that all things work together as one? All things are with Divine Purpose and Divine Plan? Is there one there to tempt you? And is there no need to take the test as it is perceived? Would you be able to take this test at this time with an honest heart? Do you understand? We have brought all to this classroom at this time. All are coming to the classroom to take this wondrous test, this wondrous growing in belief of mankind. As we have said, many are called, but few will answer. Do you not see this test?

Question: "Yes. Is there any sign that we will know that the Earth Changes are happening? Edgar Cayce gave a timetable, as did others, such as, first Earth destruction, like volcanoes, storms?"

I would like to say to you the Golden Light within the sky is the first sign, the Golden Light that shines with eight rays.

Question: "The Golden Light, is that like an Aura above the planet?"

I am not permitted, at this time, to give you more but I would say to you, the Golden Light which shines within the sky is that of eight rays.

Question: "I'd like to ask about the local area, here where we live, will it be disrupted very much?"

We would like to impart the knowledge to you of advance consciousness and the effect of mass consciousness upon the organism known as Earth at this time. If we were to give a reading, reflecting the mass consciousness, you would see much destruction upon the coastal line. However, at the time of the critical shake or shift, as we have spoken of, do you not see this is reflective to mass consciousness, as it is tied to that of the organism known as Earth?

Question: "So then, how people think around us will either protect us or destroy us?"

No, it is not how people think, it is how people are. You see, it is the vibration that comes from the heart, that which is the integral process of the Beloved I AM Presence. The I AM, the Higher Self, which comes and lives within the heart of man, which is the embodiment of the Christ Spirit, coming to live inside of man.

Question: "So it is totally up to us, whether or not things are destroyed?"

It is totally up to you to obtain your eternal freedom. I will speak of destruction. There is a synthesis of fear, fear which has no place within the integration of the Christ Spirit and mankind. Fear furthers the separation of man and the Source.

Question: "There need be no fear whatsoever?"

There need be no fear whatsoever, for if your heart is totally integrated with that of the Highest Self, the I AM Presence, are you not enfolded within the loving, nurturing hands of your Parents?

Question: "Makes sense. Then, in order to help Mother Earth to heal, will prayer help?"

Not only will it heal the Earth, it will heal you. And this is what we are most concerned about. It is more important that we not specifically ask for the healing of the Earth, for her healing is assured. It is more important that we look at the healing of those that occupy the Earth, those that are on the Earth Plane.

Question: "So we are like a disease on Mother Earth at times?"

If you will perceive yourself as being as such, however the Christ Light lives within you. How could this be perceived as a disease? This is not so. You are a great light. You are one who was brought forth to manifest this light, to let it grow and expand out to your Brother and to your Sister, a great light which all may become one day. Do you understand?

Response: "Yes."

And so we seek the way we may come to this point of knowing within our heart that which is true, that which is known as discernment. I have said to you, to know yourself, to know yourself well, to take the necessary steps to become the individualized part of God that you are. Become ONE together, individualized from the Source and yet ONE with the Source. And so you take an individual path, that which seems to work the easiest for you. And you come to this point, of becoming one of many upon the path, one collected into your soul cluster known as the twelve gene pools. You come as one collective to this point, a point of unity.

Question: "Why are so many people physically ill at this time?"

They are running away from that which has come to serve them. Do you not see the human creation, not only through the physical creation but also the mental creation is that which we must rise through, pierce through, rise above. Disease, as you have understood as dis-ease, not being at ease with the path one has chosen, one has become dis-integrated with the Source. And so, we have many who resist this great leap of the Flame of the Source that is coming to the hearts of man at this time. We have many who are not willing to take the necessary steps and allow the Source to work with them. Many do not feel that the Source is within them, a part of them and what is due them. It works as an electro-magnetic current would work through a cord, as a conductor. You must perceive yourself as a conductor of this great energy Source, not one who stands separate and away from it, but one that it runs through in a continuous flowing of current.

Question: "So, if we do what we are drawn to do, listen to what we are guided to do, we will be well? If we open and allow the God Source to lead our lives, then we will be well?"

I did not say "to lead your lives" but to direct your life, for I have said, we are to become individualized. You are to choose, you are to discern, you are to reach, if you will. We are not here to be set away and apart from you but we are here to be your Brothers, to feast with you, to sup with you, to become with you. We will not tell you the way to do it; however, we will be there to serve you, to assist you, to help you. We are here to help you attain.

Question: "Thank you. Are there any messages you wanted to give us? We have been concerned as to how we can feel more secure with this information and to never instill fear."

We have given this information to you to disseminate to those who are willing, to those who have the ears to hear and the eyes to see. It is the message to you to trust, to learn to trust.

Question: "Are we putting information out in a way that's pleasing to you or could we do more."

Of course, we would always hope that more is done but we understand, with that of a human personality, that which is done. We are most pleased and give our thanks for the work that has been done. We extend our thank you for all who have touched this work and all who have brought their insight and light to this work. This work will continue for those who have eyes to see and ears to hear. It is important to take all the doors that open and it is important to see that the Light of God never fails. The lesson is that of trust, to trust in that which we send and to trust in that which you see.

Question: "We would ask you at this time, if you would please help and look over us and guide us, so that the work would be done in the proper path."

We will guide and direct this work at all times. We send our message of love and peace and ask that all information be presented to instill hope to mankind, for an age is upon us, an age which comes to enlighten, not only the mind of man but to enlighten the heart.

3

The Cellular Awakening instigates a movement of positive,
spiritual energy that can change our physical bodies.

Free Motion
Saint Germain

Before the children arrive for summer, I have one final tour in the Northwest. This will be a new and difficult experience, as I will present the Map by myself, and after my presentation, I feel invigorated and energized by the message of the Spiritual Teachers. My shaman friend Paul continues to support me to "take my power," and to not hold back. The Map needs my presence, he says, not only as its messenger, but also because of my female energies. Since the Map's message is innately masculine, the feminine tempers and softens the edges of its prophetic wisdom.

First stop is Wenatchee, Washington, where I present the material to a New Age center. Afterwards a high-school classmate walks up to say "hi." It isn't unusual that I would meet an old classmate, but I find it astounding that she would actually attend my talk and embrace the ideals of this message—we both grew up in a very conventional, conservative small town. I learn that her spiritual awakening, brought on by different life circumstances than mine, nearly mirrors the timing of mine. A few days later in Port Townsend, I meet another old acquaintance, and the story is so similar. Clearly, there is a universal energy that is moving many people at this particular time to spiritually awaken.

After my final talk in Seattle, I am approached by a literary agent who is interested in networking and possibly distributing the Map. Melinda invites me to display the Map at her booth at the Whole Life Expo in San Francisco in exchange for my help at her booth. I immediately agree, and within a week I'm on a plane departing for San Francisco.

Before I leave, however, I have a quick session at Sherry's. It is obvious that Saint Germain notices my shift in consciousness, both mentally and emotionally. This he terms the "Cellular Awakening." The Cellular Awakening prepares our consciousness to accept the movement of positive emotion to awaken our cellular memory of spiritual divinity and the innate ability to co-create. Apparently, as we evolve through the Cellular Awakening, our entire energy system is susceptible to change. This involves not only the Chakra System and energy fields, but allegedly impacts our physical cells and DNA.

Greetings from the Spiritual Hierarchy. It is with great joy that we are able to share with you today and we have much work to do, for the preparation of the planet has begun. And as you perceive that which has been set up as time warp or Time Compaction, you must understand that this so-called timing is at hand and is part of what you have called predestination. For America, as you call the land upon which you live, is a country preordained to hold what is called the Cup of Light.

I send to you a message of peace, this peace to be held within your heart. As I have said to you, the organism known as the Earth is awakening, not only to that which you call, individually, the cellular memory. The planet, itself, is awakening to its own call. She is awakening to her own cellular memory and awakening to the purpose she serves. She has a destiny serving as a great light, a place that people, entities of like force, come to move through and walk through the energy vibration you refer to as emotion. For yes, it is true that the soul's growth and greatest gain has always come through that vibration called emotion.

Emotion impresses upon the cellular memory, for Cellular Awakening does not occur through mental activity. However, mental activity assists the awakening. Cellular memory or Cellular Awakening does not occur through physiology, in terms of that which is acted upon the body. However, it assists greatly and we recommend its use. But the greatest force to awaken the cellular memory is through allowing emotion to move. And yes, you have many definitions of emotion but we are speaking of the e-motion as a motion.

You have experienced many emotions, those of lust, greed, sadness, and sorrow, which you have perceived as pain. And there are emotions of joy, laughter, happiness, that which you have perceived as being good and light-hearted. However, the movement through these, which you perceive as emotion, is neither good nor bad, for it is movement through that the cells are jostled and turned. It is the Christ Spirit which is speaking to the self, "Awake and join me. Awake and become ONE with me."

Let me explain this in a technical manner. We refer to light harmonics and their influence upon the body and the mind and how they scatter and jostle that within the cell. This brings forth an awakening of such, so that emotion begins to flow through the body. And yet, when I refer to the body, I'm speaking specifically to that of the spiritual body, for you must understand, emotion running through Spirit is as water or oxygen moving through the human physiology and is that which feeds it and gives it life and light, preparing it for Co-creation with the God Source.

In human physiology there are several colors that you understand associated with light harmonics for Cellular Awakening and cellular memory. There is cobalt blue and another vibration, which is gold. Within gold is a structure, much similar to the structure you would understand as Cellular Awakening or cellular memory, allows freedom of motion throughout your spiritual body. For you see, congestion of the Spirit causes congestion of the physiology and mental capability. This, in turn, allows disintegration of the physical vehicle.

Our purpose on the Earth Plane and Planet at this time is to bring forth that which integrates all for free movement, free flowing, or free motion, as you call it. What we would prefer to call that which you have termed emotion, is free motion, motion to move in and out of all that is contained within universal knowledge and principle. I understand your limitation in dealing with the physical and mental body at this time, to understand the concept of free motion. However, it is our hope, through our assistance and imparting technical knowledge, you come to grasp an understanding through the mind. To grasp this and take it and move with it, motion with it, or go with it, as you would say, will produce a flow into free motion.

Saint Germain is introducing a piece of technology aimed to assist one in the integration of the energy points of the body, mind, and spirit (Chakra Centers) to assist the free movement of emotional energy. The device is a rod, containing small cylinders inside of it. Much of the technical information regarding this rod is left out at this time; however, I would like to share the information surrounding its use.

I would like to speak about free motion in relationship to what you have termed DNA, that which is genetic memory. I would like to suggest, at this time, that you allow your concepts and mental perception of DNA and genetic memory to be pushed aside momentarily, for cellular memory is closely associated with that which you would understand as Godhead, the Source of Creation, the Source of being. Your concept of DNA and genetic memory is associated with that source of limitation of I am because I am, versus cellular memory stating strongly, I AM THAT I AM. Do you see the difference? And this perception, I present to you at this time, is the eighth center, an energy point of the body representing what we call The Awakening.

You have studied much of the so-called energy centers of the body, the Chakra System, and we introduce to you the eighth point, the Awakening Point. This involves the integration of all energy points into one and forms a point of reference. Three to four yards, as you call them, from what is called the heart center and three to four yards from your crown center, extends in pyramidal shape and performs a function known as the Eighth Triad.

The point of the Eighth Triad functions as an energy apex, joining that of like cellular memory to like cellular memory. It calls from itself like a beacon, a lighthouse in the fog, calling out to join with that which is the Source. This is reflected in others of like harmonic vibration and also joins with that of like harmonic Vibration of the Cellular Awakening of the Earth Planet. So, you feel directed to be physically located in one spot and feel directed to be located in Spirit with those who also have manifested this point, to draw to itself that of the same. As I give to you technical and instructive advice, perhaps I shall state this most simply, as I have throughout much of my teaching, the use of the Violet Flame. Mercy and Forgiveness, as it flows through you, is again the highest principle of which I speak. It is hard for you to perceive that something so simple, ordained as plain, could achieve such miraculous and marvelous results. However, we understand your need for symbols and bring them to you with love for the condition of humanness. I send to you an affirmation in decree form.

I AM loved.
I AM awakened to my true being.
I AM loved.
I AM a part of my whole being.
I AM loved.
I AM ONE within that love.

I AM yours, Saint Germain.

4

*Develop trust and acceptance of self. This helps one to find peace, joy,
and laughter, which initiates Cellular Awakening—a timely means of
spiritual evolution, a precursor of the Ascension Process.*

Rapture and Ascension

Saint Germain
Sananda
Kuan Yin
Paul

I arrive for the Whole Life Expo in San Francisco. I'm traveling with the literary agent Melinda and her husband, and after landing at the San Francisco airport, we shuttle over to our room, just blocks away from the convention center. I will room with Barbara Marx Hubbard, a well-known futurist and keynote speaker at the expo. I mentioned this to Paul before I left, and his mouth literally dropped open. "Do you know who she is?" he asked. "She is literally one of the key leaders of the New Age movement and the founder of the conscious evolution movement . . . I have known about her for years . . . do you have any idea how amazing this is?" Paul then added, "See what you are attracting? Everything in your life is changing."

To be perfectly honest, I didn't know who she was. So I scrambled to the New Age section of the local bookstore and found that if the New Age had a modern-day mother, it would be Barbara. She was a contemporary of Buckminster Fuller and would later be featured in a biography by author Neale Donald Walsch.

I spent the first day of the expo helping set-up Melinda and Barbara's booth and wove my way throughout the aisles of vendors featuring everything from psychic readers to aura photography. I immediately became friendly with another volunteer at our booth—Jan—and had lunch with the psychic reader in the next booth over, who lived in Sacramento. This was definitely a place where I belonged. There was no explaining or apologies needed when someone asked, "And what do you do?" I could readily declare, "I'm a clairaudient trance channel." No one asked, "What is that?" rather, "Who do you channel?"

I had just finished hanging an I AM America Map on the wall of the booth, with a sign taped on it: "$15," when a Native American man stopped by and spent almost ten minutes viewing the coastlines with great interest. He silently poured over the Map and then intently asked me, "Is this yours?" "Yes," I replied and I went onto to explain a few of the prophecies from my presentation and how I had originally received the information. He then went into great detail about the prophecies of his Native people—the Maya. I listened to his compelling story and how he believed that one day we humans might experience catastrophic Earth Changes or experience a shift in human consciousness. Our prophecies shared profound and innate parallels. He pulled a five-dollar bill out of his pocket and asked me, "Would you sell me a copy for five dollars?" "Of course," I replied, and handed him a freshly rolled print and placed a rubber band around it. I noticed a sparkle in his eyes, obviously happy that he got a deal on the Map.

Jan ribbed me as he walked away, "Do you know who that was?" "Uh, no . . ." Boy, I was beginning to feel sophomoric. "That was Hunbatz Men. He is a famous Maya teacher and elder." And she pointed to the program catalog, where I learned he was yet another keynote speaker. Later that afternoon we stood on a balcony overlooking the stage where he danced, dressed in colorful feathers in traditional Maya ceremonial attire.

On the last day of the conference, a young gentleman with sandy blond hair and eyes the color of the sky stopped by to ask if he could speak with Barbara. "I'm sorry, she's not here right now . . . can I leave a message for her?" His attention was diverted to the Map and after several minutes of perusing the copy, he turned to me. Our recognition was instant, like the first glimpse of a cherished friend after years of separation. "What do you think is the real message of this Map?" His question was undoubtedly provocative, and as he stared at me with a laser-like focus, his gaze literally opened a hidden door in my soul, and a wave of emotion overcame me and my eyes filled with tears, "This Map is to awaken us to our divine purpose." Surely, he too felt the pure rush of energy—revealing a layer of unknown soul stratum and an indescribable, silent moment of connection.

"Are you staying with Barbara?" he asked while he purchased a Map. "Yes," I responded, a bit embarrassed by my raw, yet sincere reaction. "Would you tell her that David stopped by?"

David walked off with his rolled Map under his arm, and again Jan filled me in on the salient details. "Watch out for him; he's got a reputation and is quite the ladies man!"

Late that afternoon I returned to my hotel room, and surprisingly Barbara was back from her lecture. "I understand that you've met my friend David," she said, handing me a slip of paper with his phone number. "He'd like you to call him."

"Since this is your last day in San Francisco, I want to show you the town," he told me later on. And we sped through at least a dozen house-lined blocks in David's sports car, rolling over one paved hill after another on our way to the beach. Once there, we walked along the ocean for about an hour and watched the sun disappear into a Pacific pool of gold and red light.

As we sat eating dinner together at David's favorite Thai restaurant, he boldly stated, "I'm attracted to you."

No doubt, I was attracted to him too, but I wasn't sure if I was ready for any type of relationship. "You know, I have three children," I responded.

"I've raised children, and I love children," he replied.

Score, right answer . . . yet, maybe Jan was right—he was smooth.

Before I left his car parked outside my hotel room, David kissed my cheek and thanked me for the wonderful evening. Then, in a gentle voice he asked, "Will you see me again?"

"I'll think about it—I've got your number." I closed the car door and waved good-bye.

The next morning Barbara and I chatted about the channeling experience. I explained to her about how the Spiritual Teachers had appeared and given the details regarding the Map. She was eager to speak with them, and so without a monitor or a tape recorder, I tranced a quick fifteen-minute session. Saint Germain readily appeared and shared details about the innate, divine human evolutionary process— Ascension.

Returning home to Asotin, I was so excited to share all of this with Sherry I didn't know where to start. Sherry remained politely unimpressed. "You know, we're behind on our channeling schedule, and I hope we can get in several good sessions this week, especially before your kids arrive." And she added, "We're getting calls from everywhere, and they all have questions for the sessions. Glenda and Lynne will be here tonight, so see you around 7 p.m."

"Well, good-bye, San Francisco . . ." I whispered to myself as I walked out the door, "Hello *real* life."

In the following session, the Spiritual Teachers begin where they last ended, but not from the last session with Sherry—from the last session with Barbara in San Francisco. This teaching is unique, and four Spiritual Teachers come forward to offer their insights on the New Times, the Time of Change, and the great change awaiting humanity: the spiritual transcendence of Ascension. Each teacher offers a different technique to deal with the constant ever-present landscape of change that Earth and humanity are now experiencing: the Time of Transition. Saint Germain offers the alchemical wonder of both the Cellular Awakening and the Violet Flame and their ability to raise vibration and transform chaos into peace. Sananda shares physical healing techniques, and Kuan Yin reiterates the power of self-love. And the Spiritual Master Paul offers the Dance of the Flame, a self-affirmation of harmony and joy. Sometimes there is so much to absorb, and Sherry perceptively tells Saint Germain, "It is so hard to keep it steady. We get it, we keep it, and then we lose it." Saint Germain reminds us, "Beloved Sisters, hold your flame, hold it strong . . . be brave, and have courage."

And again, I repeat, "Hold your flame."

My Beloved chelas, I AM Saint Germain. I AM most happy to serve you this evening. I AM here for your assistance and further questioning. We have brought forth these members from the Council of the Tribunal. We have brought them to form the collective energy source of which we speak to you tonight. We are most happy for your diligence and care in preparation of this information and are most happy to see those who will truly serve.

We bring hope and peace, whereas you carry the message of cataclysm and Earth Changes to the public at large. It is our hope that, at all times, you restore the message of hope and peace and will also give your sense of gentleness to those who come in contact with you. We have listened to your discussion previously of encountering many who are different than you. Remember, at all times, to give to them the gentleness of your spirit, forgiveness, and mercy, for truly, what you see in another, do you not have it in yourself? Before we enter into the evening of discourse, again we ask for your permission.

Response: "Yes, you have our permission."

We are most happy to serve you. Upon the Earth Plane at this moment, there are great winds to occur. Look for major Earth Changes in the weather patterns concerning the Elemental Life Force, particularly those upon the East Coast and those within the Eastern hemisphere. Look to the direction of the East to see, for we are restoring faith and trust within you, not only faith and trust in us but faith and trust within yourself.

Beloved Sisters, hold your flame, hold it strong. We ask for you to be brave and to have courage. Do you not know that the Light of God Never Fails? It is the sincere heart that steps forward to do this work. It is the sincere heart that truly believes in itself. It is through this Vibration of Sincerity and through this Vibration of Worship, this Divine Quality which you have brought to this service that you do this work upon this planet and we are most happy for your diligent service. We send our blessings and love and extend our peace to you.

You see, Dear ones, Dear Children of this Flame of the Light of God, do you see that it is internal peace that is our goal? Do you not see that it is internal peace and extending this to your external world of chaos? This is our mission, for we cannot proceed in our harvest, we cannot proceed in the Ascension, until you have balanced yourself and brought the momentum of peace. Peace comes to one, not through external doing; peace comes to one through internal being, internal acceptance, and also internal joy and laughter. Peace is not extreme. Peace is not an emotion. Peace is the state of moving through the human emotion and finding within the mental states and through the mental states, the point of being to accept the self. You have your questions, Dear one, please proceed.

Question: "First of all, I'd like to ask about a friend who's working with us, who's putting this information out in a book. He wants so much to get in touch with you; he wants to feel your Presence; he wants to know that you will guide him, so that he makes no error when he puts out the information on paper and readies the book. He would like to know, would you agree to work with him?"

Of course, we extend our hand to all who ask. It is the diligent service that brings one to this path. We are most happy to extend our help to him. It is important that he seek us through prayer and meditation, also through the affirmation, "I AM in service to the Light of God that Never Fails, I AM in service to mankind, I AM in service to the self of the flame." We extend our greeting to this light force, this great light force, who has stepped forth as a being of light and send him our blessing.

He's standing, his hand on his heart. He has his other hand out and there are two lights that are streaming from his hand. There is a violet light and a gold light. Sananda is joining him, doing the same. There is a pink light and a green light that is flowing.

We send these four Rays of Love: Green, the ministration of self, for self healing, Pink, the ministration of self for self love, Violet, transformation within the self, to bring forth directed purpose, and Gold, the synthesis of being, an acceptance of self in service. You see, Dear ones, it is the service that you extend to others that affords you the opportunity to raise your vibration through the Cellular Awakening. We have spoken much about the Cellular Awakening and again extend the message that it too works upon the ministration of these four Rays, working cohesively as one. For you see, it has been said, as you extend yourself to others, you too indeed receive.

It is important that he be open to receiving. He has long felt that he was not open to receive these gifts that come. There are three people within his life and he has not accepted their healing force. They have a need to extend this to him to receive their own personal sense of healing. Do you not see how this works together in a harmonious fashion? It is important that for him to receive, he must receive from others. Please extend this message to our comrade and Brother and give him our thanks, for we are willing and ready to hand him the gift.

Question: "Would it be all right to ask that you give him some kind of sign when you are there, so that he knows?"

We will send the sound vibration of the 8.6, which works upon the E vibration. He will identify with this. We will also extend these four Rays and ask for him to be open to receive four gifts.

Response: "We thank you, thank you very much."

Question: "I'd like to ask for one who says he is trying so hard to get his body to produce immuno-globulins and it is not working."

This feeling of the Cellular Awakening has been brought within his light-field; Beloved Sananda would like to step forth for the cosmic healing.

My beloved Sister, I AM Sananda and I AM most happy to serve you. Do you not see, Dear one, the acceptance of self is that which is at stake in this case? The healing force of the hands should be used much in this case. Do you not see light force streaming forth from your hands?

He's holding out his hands.

We ask for you to receive this gift from us, hold your hands forth. Beloved Sister, you have received this, take this and apply this with your hands. Remember, the healing force.

Response: "I can feel it."

I will instruct you, Dear one, in the use of this energy vibration. It flows from the end of the index finger, the primary vibration coming forth and forming a web of energy and an electronic substance throughout the ends of the fingertips. This comes forth from what you call the universal supply. This will prevent the stoppage, the blockage, and maintain balance within his light field, particularly around the throat and ear area. We ask for you to extend this gift to your beloved Brother.

Response: "Thank you very much."

I AM most happy to serve you. I AM Sananda and leave you in joy and peace.

My Beloved Sister, I come to you, I AM Kuan Yin. I speak to you of your Beloved mate. You have given him of your gifts and we ask for you to give the gift to yourself. For long, you have given much to many and to others and you have received much from this. We ask for you to surround yourself with light and love for yourself. We ask for you, Beloved Sister, to see the light within your own self. To see this within yourself and hold it close to you, to bring it forth and nurture it as you would a child within your womb. You have questions about this light within yourself. We assure you, Dear one, it is real. Let it come forth in full self-acceptance. Do you not see that you are our Beloved? Do you not see how cherished you are? We are so thankful that you have come to be with us and bless you in radiance and peace.

My Beloved Sister, it is the dance of joy that you have brought to this planet and we are most happy that you continue this Dance of Flame with us. I AM Beloved Paul and will introduce myself to you as a dancing flame of joy. I have been with you and will remain with you through many of the days to come. In all that you do, see laughter. In all that you do, see joy. In all that you do, see the sweet music that has been strung in front of you. See the sweet music of these people that come to you, each a different note in this orchestra that is playing, each that works and harmonizes to form the sheet music that is in front of you, to play this great orchestra that you are to conduct. See yourself this way, as a composer of music and see this great piece before you and hear its song, so masterful and sweet it seems to you. I AM Paul, I AM the Flame of Joy. Come forth in brilliance, come forth in radiance. We thank you for the work you do and we prepare you for the greater work before you.

Saint Germain steps forward.

As we come forth to you, you too come forth to us. Let us deepen our commitment in service and dance in the joy of humanity. Let us laugh at the silly things that are said and done and let us have great joy, for are not all of these personalities but that of the Source? Does not God express in many ways? Are there not many flowers in the garden? Are there not many trees that cover your beautiful Earth Planet that has brought herself forth for you? Are there not many rivers? Are there not many songs? And each brings their collective unit. See this and be with it and enjoy it. We ask for you to work to your fullest.

Question: "Thank you. Could you explain what the word "rapture" means?"

Rapture means the acceptance of Ascension.

Question: "And could you explain what Ascension means?"

Astral travel does not achieve this. Astral travel is the ability to use the mental mind/body to move within the light field. Ascension uses all bodies.

Question: "You can then take the body, just as you are, and walk from one dimension to the other?"

This is correct. This commands: I AM THAT I AM. It is a command from the Word, the Source, the Logos, the Creative Force. I AM THAT I AM, remember this, Dear ones. It is forceful enough for you to make your Ascension on this scientific formula alone. I AM THAT I AM, remember this, Dear hearts. Combine this with the Violet Flame, of which we have brought instruction for your use for Purity, for Forgiveness, for Mercy, for Compassion, for Transformation.

Question: "It is so hard to keep it steady. We get it, we keep it, and then we lose it. It's real hard to keep it in our lives every day."

We understand, Dear one. Laugh. Use laughter to look at the self. This removes the sense of judgment of self.

Response: "Judgment's the biggie."

It is the denier of self.

Question: "When things go wrong and the Earth starts changing, many people seem to want it to happen."

Beloved, it is the purification, it is the cleansing.

Question: "On all levels?"

On all levels.

Question: "Many people want to change the structure of things and the government."

This government you speak of is changing, purifying, and refining.

Question: "It is changing, the same as the Earth is changing, and the same as people are changing?"

All levels are purifying and in transition.

Question: "And it's changing according to our mass consciousness?"

Of course, the mental state affects the purification. It is only the acceptance of the purification. The mental state is that which comes forth to perceive, to function, for how can you purify the body and spirit, you see, without the mental body? Again, I give you a formula, $E=mc^2$.

My Beloveds, I take leave this evening and send you a blessing of peace. Beloved ones of the Flame, dance in Violet Fire.

5

We are individually developing and spiritually working with
the Universal Mind that inevitably merges to ONE mind.

The Extended Will

Saint Germain
Mary
Kuan Yin
Soltec

I receive a letter from Dr. Chet Snow, the author of *Mass Dreams of the Future*—a collection of hundreds of people's experiences that describe their journeys into future lives through the use of hypnosis. He has written to ask if I could meet him at the Whole Life Expo next month in San Diego. I am especially eager to meet Dr. Snow as his book is based upon research with the late Helen Wambach, who shared her groundbreaking studies in reincarnation and past-life recall in her book, *Life Before Life*, a dog-eared favorite in my library. Dr. Snow also includes evidence in his book regarding possible upcoming Earth Changes as we enter the twenty-first century and their relationship to a profound human evolutionary transformation. Sherry is adamant that I go, and after asking the Spiritual Teachers about the trip, they insinuate that this trip will be vital for networking the Map.

In the meantime, David and I have talked at least a dozen times in two weeks and our friendship is quickly evolving into a personal relationship. He assures me, "No matter what happens in our relationship, I always want to be your friend, first." His words are reassuring, especially since the break-up with Dan.

David is also a seasoned student of the Ascended Masters, and in his early years he thoroughly absorbed Alice Bailey's material. He constantly asks me questions about Saint Germain, the Golden Cities, and how to apply this new information in context to all that he has previously read. Spiritually, he is one of the most evolved and thoughtful people I have ever encountered, and I am undeniably captivated.

In one of our night-long conversations, we fervently debate freewill and conclude that this notion evaporates as our spiritual evolution progresses into group effort. Alice Bailey refers to this crucial development as the "Externalization of the Hierarchy," that is, we begin to mirror the Spiritual Teachers' great cause for humanity. One night David reads one of Bailey's inspiring invocations:

"Let the Forces of Light bring illumination to mankind.
Let the Spirit of Peace be spread abroad.
May men of good will everywhere meet in a Spirit of Cooperation.
May forgiveness on the part of all men be the keynote at this time.
Let power attend the efforts of the Great Ones.
So let it be, and help us to do our part."

I swear that the Spiritual Teachers must listen in on our conversations, both physically and telepathically, and in the next session, the subject of freewill is the first topic Saint Germain presents. In this lesson, the individualized freewill is said to contribute a creative spark to the group mind, which in turn is nurtured and cared for by the group mind. The Spiritual Teachers metaphorically compare the relationship of group mind to freewill to how a family or tribe cares for each individual member. Saint Germain describes this model as the Extended Will. Three more Spiritual Teachers join the discussion and share information on diet and food storage for the Time of Change, and as usual, answer our everyday questions.

Welcome, Beloved chelas, I AM Saint Germain. I have come this day to give you further instructions. I will serve tonight as facilitator and would like to introduce to you the quorum that surrounds me, a quorum of three, that of Beloved Mary, Beloved Kuan Yin, and that which you have known as Soltec, who is also here to give the technical expertise that you have questions about. I AM here for your assistance and as I have introduced the quorum to you, you may also address them as they step forward to give their insight. I would also like to say at this time, that we are not allowed to infringe upon your freewill and seek your permission at all time to give assistance. Do we have the approval of all those present?

Question: "Yes. Is that what you mean about your freewill?"

This is precise, for we are not allowed to infringe upon the freewill, not only of that of the human, but that which is the individualized Christ Light, for you see, you are one of the same Source and yet you are individualized. You become ONE with the Source and while an individual, you are not separated. See the many flowers in the garden. There are many colors and many varieties to choose from and yet they all comprise a garden. But you may choose a specific flower. Do you understand?

Response: "Yes."

We are most thankful to be here and happy to serve you. For you see, Dear ones, it is the service of the light that is of the highest order and you must see yourself as an extension of that light, as one who is becoming increasingly more aware of that. We beg of you to call to us, for we gladly give our assistance to you. You may understand us as that of the inner direction, however, our work is in a different perspective. Our work with you is that of radiating energy, for as we send the Ascended Master radiating energy to you, you are able to fine tune into what you call the inner self, the connection in the Heart Chakra area to that of the Higher Self, your own mighty I AM Presence. We, through your approval, may send to you the radiating substance which allows this to be enhanced. Do you understand?

Question: "Is this turning your life over to God?"

You can turn your life over to this energy source to become a member of the family. Perhaps the way to explain this to you, in a way that you may understand in human form, is to understand the family unit. For as you go into your collective groups, that which has been known as a family, you enter with specific rules and guidelines. Are you not entering into agreement with this family? You see this extended throughout all family or tribal members or societal members. You have indeed turned your will, as you understand it, that which is the extended will, over to that source. And so we have that which is the extended will, that which is cared for and nurtured by members of the tribal family. And then we have that which is the individualized will. The individualized will is that which seeks to become an individualized, creative energy source. For you see, Dear ones, each serves their part and each is an integral part of the tribal or family unit. Do you understand?

Question: "Yes. I would now like to ask about the microwave, what it does to our food and if it harms the food, making it so that it isn't good for our bodies?"

I would like to introduce to you, my Brother Soltec, who will step forward to answer your specific questions.

Greetings from the Diamond Heart, I AM Soltec. I come from the Golden Ray, that which is coming, that which you understand as predestined. You are speaking of rearrangement of the molecular structure with the use of the microwave. I would like to place in front of you a diagram.

He is drawing a honeycomb shaped cell. It has six sides and at the end of it, it elongates out to a point and there are other points, they all join on that. They all come together and form a massive ball.

The process that we would like to explain to you is to show how all parts of a whole become separated and disjointed. You have concern over the issue surrounding foodstuffs, heating in particular, for the rearrangement of this creates what is called a kellular energy source.

He's showing the kellular energy source. It comes from the center.

As the kellular energy source is broken apart, from the rotation of the six-sided cells, the kellular energy expands to the outside surface and yes, there are some toxins that occur from this. You have been correct in your assumption. However, it is at a level that is tolerable at this time. However, as you enter into higher vibration, it is important that you limit your intake of such foods that have been rearranged. We would recommend high use of that which you have known as water, to flush the kellular toxins from your systems.

Question: "Is that what they call free-radicals?"

You may know it as free-radicals but we call it the kellular toxins, which have a tendency to adhere to what is known as the Solar Plexus Chakra Center. We would recommend, as you enter into higher light activity, the use of raw foods, for not only are they flushing, they are nourishing to this Chakra Center. Do you understand?

Question: "Yes. Are there other things we can do to make the Time of Change go easier on the physical plane?"

My dear, there is much that can be done, if only there were bodies to do and ears to hear, eyes to see. There is much to do on the physical and there is much to do on the mental. The far-reaching work is that of the emotional cleansing. However, there are many preparations which can be made at this time. It seems ludicrous, I am sure, to build a hut of mud, only to have the foot put upon it. But there are technologies to be dispensed and ways which this cleansing can come forth with great ease and enlightenment, particularly that of foodstuffs and food preparation. If only man would realize that all he needs is present in universal substance. Yes, we are speaking of precipitation and this will not be a miracle in the times to come, this will not be a phenomena. However, the public at large, ninety-nine percent to be more precise, is unaware and made unavailable to this. And so, we would suggest the use of food stuffs that are vacuum-packed, those that do not contain air or water substance, and those which are light and easy to carry.

Question: "Do you mean freeze-dried?"

Yes, that which is also available is powdered-form.

Question: "Dehydrated and gas packed?"

Precisely. We would suggest the collecting and storing of such for a two-year supply. Not just for yourself, but to share with your Brother, for you see, as the increased energies radiate to the planet, you will be using less and less of that which you have known as food energy and drawing upon that which has been referred to as the universal, or in other verbiage, know as Prahna.

Question: "So, we won't need to eat after a while, as much?"

As much, my Dear, however, as long as you are in physical embodiment, water is necessary and the intake from the universal.

Question: "There is an energy here in this residence that's affecting the people who live here, particularly their teeth. Can you tell me what that's about? What's causing that?"

With the teeth, there is an over abundance of calcium in the system and we recommend a small dosage of such, also, a higher proportion of oxygen to the system.

Question: "Where is the vibration coming from?"

We are unaware of such at this time, however we would be glad to research this and send it to others to bring you back further information.

He is getting information from someone.

The vibration you are feeling in your teeth is specifically related to that of sonar, that of the ear, that of the hearing. There is a resonance around what is known as the Crown Chakra, extending into a residence of B-flat, which has come to the planet from a Solar System yet to be discovered.

Question: "Is there a way that we can adjust that vibration so that it is not toxic?"

My Dear, it is not toxic, it is different. You must adjust to the frequency, so it does not interfere with your earthly body. As we encounter that which is different, it may feel toxic. We feel fear, we feel attacked, and we feel these many energy movements. However, this comes from that which is the highest source of the mental mind. It is a fine-tuned adjustment mental energy. It is not emotional based, it is not physically based, it is that which is in alignment with mental energy.

Question: "So, now that we're acquainted with that energy, we won't make it wrong and won't have to manifest the physical symptoms to explain it?"

We are developing and working upon that of the Universal Mind, that which merges all to ONE Mind. Do you understand?

Response: "Yeah…got it. Thank you."

Thank you.

He's stepping back. Saint Germain is coming up.

We send our love and blessings to Beloved Brother Soltec, for the information he has imparted to you. It is his intent to deliver the message of Golden Technology throughout this Time of Transition and he has petitioned that he may come forth to assist those who call to him. May I assist you, Dear hearts?

Question: "I would like to find out about the focus for Lori in San Diego?"

She is well aware that there were four more contacts which were not completed. There are three which are waiting, one which is still in motion and will occur on the last day. There are those who are prepared to spread this information and the work of the Masters through this vibration.

Question: "So, she will make many contacts there?"

We will assist her as she is willing.

Question: "Do you find that another map is necessary to build; the World Map, maybe, or the Greening Map?"

It is a willing heart that comes forward to serve in this capacity, one which is sensitive to that of the Mother, that which is known as Terra. As you have understood, it is a sensitive subject and if a heart is so willing to come forth, we will gladly assist.

Question: "Am I capable of helping do the work on the map?"

He is laughing!

Response: "Oh great! He always laughs at me."

Are you not doing this work, my Child? Are you not doing it at this moment, capable, willingly, lovingly? We send you our blessings and thanks for your assistance in this work. As we have said, many are called but few have answered. Do you question that you have answered?

Response: "No, just whether I am capable."

My Dear, we are humbled to serve you.

Question: "I would like to ask you what the most important thing to focus upon in the work right now? Should we put the maps in the book or should the maps be separate?"

The message of love, the message of love is the most important. Carry this through all the work and the Light of God will Never Fail, for the message of love is the thread that weaves us all together, ONE to the plane, ONE to the planet, ONE to the universe. This is a simple message indeed and yet the most exquisite, the most wondrous, the most majestic. It is that which brings joy in all you do. It is that which brings much peace to the external and internal will, as we have discussed. The work of love is of vast importance.

Question: "Are you saying that it makes no difference which medium is used, so long as the message of love is gotten out?"

This is precise! There are many ways that this message is sent and the task of Earth Change, which we are all aware of, is one that attracts many within the Vibration of Fear. Do you not see, the healing work before you? I would like to introduce my Beloved Sister Kuan Yin.

My Beloveds, take your mask off and come to me with your heart open and ready to receive, for my message of compassion for the Earth Plane. Do you see how she weeps? Do you see her disjointed? Do you see hysteria? It is time to go forth among as many as you can and extend your love to one another. I AM a being of compassion. I AM a being of love. Do you see this? I call to you to extend my work, to not only those within your groups, but go to all. Go to all and send this message.

6

Everything that is alive vibrates.
Every vibration impacts life on Earth.

The Web of Creation
Saint Germain

My trip to San Diego is extremely uplifting, and I'm able to share the Map with many lightworkers and networkers. I share the Map with Dr. Snow and he comments that it closely mirrors his research in future-life progression. Perhaps one of the most interesting people I meet is Dr. Fred Bell. I can't help but notice him at his booth sporting his famous pyramid headgear and when I show him the Map, he immediately mentions the Pleiadian time traveler Semjase. Dr. Bell was allegedly contacted by Semjase and the geography of the I AM America Map—specifically, the Mount Shasta peninsula—resembles maps used by extraterrestrial time travelers to navigate the future Earth. He invites me to a party that evening, but I opt to stay in and order room service.

My travels lead me into San Francisco where I stop for several days with David at his condo in Mill Valley. We go shopping for organic food at the market, bring home fresh salmon, and cook dinner with pictures of the Dalai Lama, Buddha, Saint Germain, and Mighty Victory peeking at us from every corner. On David's day off we go for a hike in the Muir Woods. "This is one of my favorite places," David remarks as we sit down next to a soaring, lustrous redwood. "I knew a woman who could touch a tree, and its Spirit would channel messages to her." I reach out and pat the tree, and there is no message I can decipher, yet I see the radiant energy of the elemental that protects it. This magnificent being is almost as tall as the tree and shines with glints of silver light.

That evening I receive the lesson, *Web of Creation*. This session starts with a prayer of thanksgiving to recognize and bless the creative forces of Mother Earth.

Welcome, I AM Saint Germain. I come this day to give you a message of peace for the planet, a message which is brought to you from the Logos, that which is the center of Creation.

I have returned. I AM peace.
I have come this day in love and goodwill to mankind.
I have returned. I AM the light. I have come this day to bond to you.
I have returned. I AM Creation, the inner spark from which you came.
I have returned. I AM.

Dear ones, we bring this prayer in joy and thanksgiving and send our blessings to you. And ask that you understand the concept of freewill of mankind. However, we are here for your willing assistance. Do we have your approval?

Response: "Yes."

You have sought information of Vortex areas and energy "V" points. I AM glad to let you know that there are many that exist upon the planet. They exist in numbers and circles of nine. There are nine specific regions which cover the Earth Plane and bring forth the energy points, nine layers and nine dimensions, as you would understand. We should start from pole to pole. For you see . . .

He's showing me the globe and he's marking off sections.

We divide the planet up, first in half, from what you perceive as the North to South pole, creating two hemispheres and again divide it in half, at your present equator, creating quadrants of the globe. And each of these sections is broken again into three parts or cells. Each quadrant contains a specific value or mathematical equation. We will start with the quadrant in your vicinity, associated with giving and forgiving. This area is closely associated with the portal, or access line, into the next level, a dimensional barrier. As you arrive within the line area, you are able to access finer and finer substances associated with the energy points. So, you have questions?

Question: "Could you address the nine dimensions or nine layers? Are they overlapping or are they vertical? How do we visualize the alignment of those with our Earth Plane? Where are the actual access points geographically?"

He's showing me this one quadrant, how you locate these energy points and then, showing at these energy points, a golden course of light, which streams, as directed from the outside. It then goes into the interior and to the outside of the corresponding points. I see a corresponding course of light from another quadrant. I think he's showing how it overlaps. They are held together through this course of light. The cord of light expands, extends, and then it encircles and continues on to other quadrants. Then, it goes through the different quadrants, growing ever larger.

Response: "It sounds like the weaving that holds the universe together, more like galactic Ray lines, not dimension Ray lines."

This is precise. This is the message which I bring, that which is known as the Galactic Web, the other dimensional web, but we call it the Logos Web, that which is the Web of Creation.

Question: "How can we specifically tie in for our own dimension, with the Logos and how do we work with the Logos Web to serve Earth?"

First, is a complete and precise mapping of each quadrant, to show these energy points, the access, the star portals, and on to the second layer. As of this point, I am not permitted to give the mathematical formula which gives the details of overlap. However, once the lower quadrants are completed, I will assist you in such.

Question: "So, is it one of our responsibilities to take this information and create a two or three-dimensional model of the quadrants and the nine dimensions?"

We would be honored for you to do this and we would be honored to assist you.

Response: "With the new computer technology, it would probably make it possible to do this graphically in a Three-Dimensional model and maybe we could tie it into a Fourth Dimension."

This would be a beautiful work, not only for the adjustment of the planet but for the adjustment of the world, which is the seed of other Solar Systems.

Response: "This would be a service to the Web of Logos and to other systems?"

As well as to the planet, to your Brothers and Sisters.

Question: "So this is one of Earth's and humanity's gifts to the Galaxy?"

This is precise. To bring this forth, to understand the part you play on the Earth, you take a cloth and woven in the cloth are many fibers, many threads, each with their different colors and specific attunement. However different are all the webs and all the threads, they are woven together to form one cloth, one surface, one fabric.

Question: "How would you language these nine dimensions? Would you give a quick census of each of the nine?"

The first one encircling the globe, PRAHANIC is the life-giving life force. The second is EVERNO, which causes motion. The third is ESHANO, which means hall of wisdom and light. The fourth is BUITSHA, the Heart.

That is as far as he goes to at this point.

Question: "Do we have correspondences in our physical body and can you empower and align with these?"

Our intent is to impart the information, so it can be used for assistance, not only for you and your Brothers and Sisters upon the planet, but of that of the cloth that is woven between your Brothers and Sisters of this planet and the Solar System. Also, so you may become aware of the essence of your energy, the source of your energy and the mass consciousness of the planet, that which we have referred to as the Earth Plane. There is also that of your vibrations, to help your Brothers and Sisters of the Galaxy and the interaction of their vibrations with you. Do you understand?

Question: "So humanity's experience on the Earth Plane, through the Logos Web, has a vibrational impact on all of life and all of life has a vibrational impact on us here on the Earth Plane. And to permit this, to have us become aware of this, obviously would encourage us to become holistic in our vibratory approach?"

This is precise. For we have said, you live in a world of willing whole spirit, that which is commitment to all and ONE to all. It is our attempt to break this apart in any way, for you to comprehend and understand.

Question: "How do we have an impact on our Brothers and Sisters throughout the Galaxy? Would you be more specific? Intent or love, just our knowing, or do we do something else?"

We would prefer for you to understand logistic locations of this nervous system we present to you. For depending which way you project a thought and also your physical presence, you are able to contact through these points of sensitivity. Does not the human body contain union? It has points of sensitivity, points of access.

Question: "Is there any point on the grid, geographically, that you would like us to go to?"

There is one in specific; however, all of them are points you may travel to through the telepathic portal, or through the physical vehicle, whichever serves you best. Thank you and bless you. And I hand to you the Flame of Life. I AM ONE with you, call to me. I AM Saint Germain.

7

The Cellular Awakening transforms both Spirit and body.

Cellular Instruction
Saint Germain
Portia
Kuthumi

I return to Asotin, happy to be home and to settle back into my routine. Before I leave San Francisco, David hands me a copy of Alice Bailey's *Great Invocation*. This world prayer was given to Bailey in 1945 by Maitreya the Christ to promote healing, cooperation, and peace among humanity. It is also alleged that Lord Maitreya gave the prayer to prepare the world for the second coming of the Christ. This spiritual tenet is a bit controversial among students of Ascended Master teachings. Some students think that the second coming of Christ is a literal appearance and that the great Master will physically appear and help to transform the world. Yet another group believes that the second coming of Christ is within each and every one of us as the Christ Consciousness. The great avatar Babaji once said, "The savior is within— reveal him."

Sherry, Glenda, and Lynne were all present for the next lesson, and before we begin, we recite the healing words of *The Great Invocation*. I definitely feel a vibrant energy in the quality of the material; perhaps you will, too.

The following lesson prophesies our entrance into Time Compaction and how this anomaly accelerates our experience of the Fourth Dimension. Another key to understanding this lesson is to digest the concept of the Eight-Sided Cell of Perfection. This is a perfect cell that the Spiritual Teachers claim is present in all human physical bodies, and it is located in our beating hearts. The perfect cell carries all the potentiality of the Godhead, and maintains a connection to our spiritual growth and evolution at this important time. Apparently the spinning of this cell at certain rates allows its replication. Yet, the Eight-Sided Cell of Perfection's most phenomenal function is its alleged ability to readjust or change DNA and ultimately transform our genetic code. This is perhaps the most important aspect of the Cellular Awakening.

We are beginning the channeling with a prayer.

> From the point of light within the mind of God,
> Let light stream forth into the minds of men.
> Let light descend on Earth.
> From the point of love within the heart of God,
> Let love stream forth into the hearts of men.
> May Christ return to Earth.
> From the center where the will of God is known,
> Let purpose guide the little wills of men,
> The purpose which the Masters know and serve...

Welcome, my Beloved Sisters, I AM Saint Germain. I AM here for your assistance and bring my message of happiness and joy to see you together as a collective unit, meeting again to meet with us. We are pleased that you are here and ready to bring service to you and as you know, ask for your permission to enter into your light field. Do we have this?

Response: "Yes."

We are ready to proceed. We are thankful that you have realized a structure to work with us and we too would like to impart the knowledge of our structure to you. As you have participated in similar discourses, or classes, as you would call them, tonight I will serve as facilitator. I AM Saint Germain, Lord of the Violet Ray—the Violet Ray which is sent to Earth at this Time of Planetary Transition. This time may be shortened due to what is called the Time Compaction Theories. As time is accelerated and the consciousness does leap into Fourth Dimensional reality, you will experience a quickening, as it is called. A quickening into the transition to Fourth Dimension consciousness is that which no longer requires the density of the Third Dimension. An acceleration of the cells of the body, as you move with that of the Christ Spirit, comes to reunite you to your mighty I AM Presence.

Tonight I would like to introduce those who have come to assist and serve you in this question and answer period and they will step forth. My Beloved Sister, Portia, who is also known as my Divine Compliment and my Brother, Kuthumi.

They are stepping forward. Kuthumi is carrying a white rose.

Tonight, we three are here for your assistance and will be glad to answer your questions. You may direct them to us and we will be most thankful to serve.

Question: "What is the significance of the white rose?"

Kuthumi is stepping forward.

To serve in purity is the highest calling of the spirit. To serve from that of the highest within, it has been set forth as a symbol brought to you. The highest motive of purity is purity of self, for purity of self opens the doors and the portals much more quickly.

Question: "How does the time warp, or the Time Compaction, affect our physical bodies?"

Saint Germain responds.

I would like to explain cellular structure to you. In front of you is an eight-sided crystalline structure which exists inside of the cell itself, rotating upon what would be perceived as a rod. With a spin associated with .317, this is the current spin rate of Third Dimension. However, with use of the Violet Flame, which encompasses the Earth Planet at this time and also that of the Earth Plane, we accelerate in increments of .063. And so, you have the spinning motion within the cell itself, the eight-sided crystalline structure, and as it spins and is accelerated bit by bit, you may add this to the acceleration. The spinning moves not only in a circular motion but in a spiral motion within the eight-sided crystalline structure.

He's drawing the diagram for it right now. He is pointing out how the axis rod that runs through the crystalline structure rotates on the spiral motion and around it is the crystalline structure that rotates on a circular basis.

Within the cell itself, is the motion of the spinning, that which is called the Cellular Awakening, that which is readjusting the DNA or genetic coding. It is also readjusting Third Dimensional mathematics, as we move into that which is Fourth Dimensional mathematics, also understood as inter-dimensional mathematics or interdimensional reality. It is essential that the body is adjusted to the Fourth Dimension reality to accommodate that of the Violet Flame Ray, or that which is known as the Galactic Beam, which is coming from the cosmos at this time to assist mankind for the higher conscious level of being. Do you understand?

Question: "Is this similar to the way the Earth, the cells within our body, and everything is then affected?"

This is correct. As we have said in all cosmic principles, "as above, so below." The same is true of your planet, for you see, the planet itself is a structure most closely associated with the cellular level of that of mankind. For man is made of earth element and therefore contains within itself the same genetic coding and also the Cellular Awakening. And so this is occurring upon the planet at this time and you may use the same mathematical code to understand areas of eruption and disintegration, for this is the message of Cellular Awakening, that it is also the disintegration of genetic coding. Do you understand?

Question: "Yes. Then if a person is already sick, is there a possibility of healing at this time? Is everything accelerated?"

Of course, my Dear, all is accelerated for the urgent call for healing. There is healing that is occurring at the physical level. However, as we have spoken of in past discourses about the concept of disease, all physical ailment is a manifestation of that which has occurred at the finer levels within that of the etheric code. For you see, within the etheric body, there are also many levels and fine adjustments to be done, seven to be exact.

Question: "How much control do we have over our own bodies and how can we help our bodies to go through this Time of Change? Are there things that we can do to make it more comfortable, so that we can attune to it sooner?"

You are speaking specifically of the body?

Response: "No, I'm also talking about our emotions and mental, our total energy."

Precisely, my Beloved Divine Compliment, Portia, would like to step forward with your permission.

Greetings, Sisters of the Flame, I AM Portia. I would like to introduce myself to you. I AM the Divine Compliment of Saint Germain, that which holds the Violet Flame Candle. Your questions are about the will and the right use of mind, for you see, Dear ones, the mental energies are also being adjusted at this time. Do you understand the separation of emotional to mental to physical and also to spiritual bodies and the finer substances and how they are affected?

Response: "It's hard for me to understand what the spiritual body is. I sometimes feel like it is part mind, part emotion."

Do you see that all these bodies are indeed an expression of Spirit. Spirit is that which threads them together and weaves them together as ONE. It is man who has perceived them as being separate and apart from one another. However, they are all part of one inclusive unit. We have the ability to let them go at will and let them manifest at will. As we have spoken about the concepts of precipitation, do you not see how an Ascended Master is able to come into the physical and take on a physical body? For you see, it is a complete manifestation empowerment of that of the knowledge of spirit. For you see, my Dear, there is no separation between each of the bodies, however there is a distinguished individuality of each, so you are able to utilize the energies of such for your use.

Question: "Can we all channel?"

There are many who are called to do this and few respond.

Question: "How can we, if we would like to channel, adjust to be able to channel? Or do we have to be called first?"

We call to all who are willing, through the conscious use of the will to raise their vibration to us; for as your vibrations are raised to us, we will lower ours to you. For you see, we love you and wish to serve you. You are indeed like our children and we are here to give service to you. There are preparations that may be done to encourage this. There are some dietary requirements, as well as that of use of the Violet Flame decrees, used at least three times per day, as we have given in past instructions. However, there are also finer subtle adjustments which need to occur in the etheric bodies, which occur during the time known as sleep to man, where energies are adjusted. It is important upon entering into the rest period to call to the Higher Self to allow your channel to open.

There is also that we call the adjustment of the Third Eye energy, that which you have known as the Third Eye Chakra. Also an adjustment of the Crown Chakra, to allow the finer energies for the leading of the body at night to go up to what we call a retreat, a place of instruction for opening to the higher energies. And understand too, when we use the verbiage of higher, we are not indicating that we come from a position that is better than you or that you are less than us. For you see, we are but an extension of you and you are an extension of us. Do you understand?

Question: "Yes. I would like to ask about the food on Earth now, is it polluted? If so, can we ask it to be cleansed when we eat it?"

You may qualify through the energies in your hand. We would say that perhaps the most qualifying energy at this time is the use of the Golden Ray. This extends, if you were to direct from the hand, through what is known as the ring finger, on the left hand side. It is a finger which specifically is in alignment with that of the Golden Ray and you may visualize from this, a band of gold light coming around from it and through the food substance that you intake. However, we agree with you, that your food is of poor quality.

Question: "Are there ways to improve that?"

There are many dietary standards which we would choose for you, so it is an easier process for us to work with you at this time. We have spoken about the use of animal products and wish for you to eliminate them entirely from your diet. However, we know your dependence on them is one which is closely associated with your genetic cellular programming. That is, for the use of the Cellular Awakening, as we have spoken of the .063 spin ratio which is occurring in your bodies at the time, you will notice a lesser and lesser desire for use of animal products. However, we would say to you, use certain foods which are in alignment with the Chakra Centers which you wish to open. Do you understand?

Question: "We have a couple of specific health needs here having to do with the cleansing of the lymph system and having to do with improving the immune system."

The cleansing of the lymph system would require the total elimination of salt from the diet. For you see, it is important to flush the system and to flush it of the mineral compounds that are found consistently in fluoride and add magnesium. However, it is also important that water, water of the highest purity, is brought into the system. Through the elimination of salt, which had allowed the retention of certain minerals within the system, we can work to flush out at this time. There is also coming into use, what is known as the archo-meter.

Question: "Is this a new purification system?"

Yes, the use of this system for no less than four times a day and also the use of water to be used during periodic cycles during the day itself. For you see, the largest amount of cleansing occurs, in most human physiology, in the morning hours, the first five hours upon waking in the morning. It is best to never consume any animal product whatsoever and particularly in these hours. For you see, my Dear ones, this is the time the etheric substance from the sleep period, or learning period, is returning to the body and it is important for the adjustment. We would suggest the use of water mixed with fruit juices, fruits that come specifically from the Golden Ray, that which would be associated with many of the fruits upon your planet, as well as a mixture of no more than one-tenth vegetable product or protein.

We take a short break and enter back into the channeling.

I AM Saint Germain. I AM Lord of the Violet Flame for this period of transition. We have spoken about the Earth and the Cellular Awakening. We have also imparted the knowledge of genetic coding to you and given you the finer mathematical calculations. We have discussed the water systems of the body and would like to impart knowledge of the fire system, that which is used through the mental capability. Through prayer and affirmation and also the will of God working in your life, you have known passion. There has been much interpretation of this word throughout the history of mankind. They have associated it with emotions centered on lust and greed. However, passion is associated with that of the Spirit and passion is that which is associated with the fire element. For you to understand this word, it is appropriate for you to understand it in its full context in your language. I would suggest for you, after our discourse this evening, to look it up and to include it in the context of this information.

PASSION: Strong amorous feeling or desire.

In imparting the knowledge of the fire element and its work within the body, we are speaking of the direct link of Spirit, the mighty I AM Presence, to that of the Heart Chakra. There are indeed certain foods that can be ingested to assist the opening of the Heart Chakra. However, the most important work is that of understanding, through the mind and use of mind, the will of your mighty I AM Presence in your life and the direction of this Presence within your waking world.

8

The illusive personality strengthens our Spirit.

The Personality

Sananda

In my beginning days with trance work, I would literally need to lie down on a couch and fall into a light, trance-like sleep. As my efforts with this technique evolved, I could physically lean on whoever was monitoring the session and enter into the meditative state. When I began to work with Sherry, she encouraged me to sit up straight in a chair and learn to sustain my energy by accepting ethereal energies supplied by the monitor or others who were sitting for the reading. Since employing these new methods, I hold the channel a bit longer, plus I have more of a conscious awareness of the material after the session is completed. However, I now need someone present to not only ask questions, but to work in some capacity as a generator.

A generator in trance work is just what the term implies. This person works both like a generator and a battery of subtle, yet invigorating ethereal energy during the session; this stream of vital energy is directed to the person in trance and allows the channeler to awake from the trance session refreshed and energized, as one might from meditation. Performing trance work without a battery present is still possible, but can be hazardous. In fact, it is claimed that not properly resting and replenishing the human energy system after channeling can be dangerous to the health of the medium. There are many reasons for this, but primarily the risks involve overloading the physical nervous system which inevitably exhausts the human energy system. This can lead to imbalances of all types, primarily health problems, disease, and in extreme cases, early death.

Yet Sherry is always pushing the envelope. In order to simplify or diversify my ability to extract insight and information from the Spiritual Teachers, she suggests that I try sessions by myself and use the energies of the Earth Mother to replenish my energy. This process is a bit like automatic-writing, but instead of using a computer or word processor, I decide to speak directly into my hand-held tape recorder.

My one and only experiment with this trance technique is featured in the next selection. While traveling for a business trip to Spokane, I took a short detour to the top of Steptoe Butte located on the perimeters of Ascension Valley in the rolling hills of the Palouse and I gave Sherry's suggestion a try. Surely my energies will quickly replenish at this ancient, sacred site, I think. The bedrock of this unique quartzite hill is over 400 million years old, and the spiritual energies are sublime.

I travel up a narrow, winding road to a parking spot and I am the only one present or perhaps more accurately expressed, the only human present. Elementals, Devas, Angels, and Spiritual Teachers all make themselves known, as I silently ground myself to the butte's majestic presence and enter into trance.

Sananda instantly appears and shares his insights on the personality and how its illusive and sometimes addictive nature can drive spiritual growth while simultaneously strengthening our Spirit with forgiveness, compassion, and love.

≫

Welcome, my Dear child, I AM Sananda. I bring to you a message of comfort, joy, and peace. For you see, the work of healing touches many upon the planet at this time and extends beyond that which reaches the global scale. It resonates from the planet itself, out to that within the cosmos. So you see, Dear ones, it touches not only the lives of those among you but touches those who will unlock another Solar System.

The personality is much to deal with. The personality is a collective force of many, many embodiments. There are embodiments that are the collective energy of many personal past embodiments. You see, as the Spirit, that which is linked with the mighty I AM Presence, densifies, it goes through the lower body. It is first to be clarified, first to become clear. Reactions are slowed down, become dense and are more easily detected and seen.

My Dear ones, the personality is not real, it is only the result of a healing force working in your life. The personality is the reactive force, the reactive force which is clearly seen. Perhaps I can help you understand this easier, to give you better clarity.

A sliver of wood embeds within your flesh and becomes sore and agitated. The wound weeps, becomes red and inflamed. The weeping, the inflammation, could be compared to that of the personality. It is not the wound itself; it is the wound in process, in process of healing. And so you see, it is much the same for Spirit. As

Spirit descends into the physical realm, taking a healing path, it would be a healing path of clarity to remove the many splinters within its nature of being. There is weeping and inflammation as this process occurs. And yet, the personality, the weeping, the inflammation that you see, is temporary. It is a temporary source, a temporary being. It serves a purpose and should be thanked and acknowledged for the gift that it gives, for it allows the skin from whence the splinter entered, to become strengthened, stronger and able to resist the penetration again by another splinter.

This collective energy, which listens only to the Spirit, beckons to the call of the Spirit and the universe responds and brings to be that which has been called forth. The Angelic Host responds and a soul enters embodiment with a personal path, a personal path that has been selected and called into motion through the universe, assisted by the Angelic Host at the Source. The Source is that, the mighty I AM Presence, that from whence the call has come, that which you have understood as the true Spirit entity of the individual.

And so, it is with great joy that you have been given your personality, yet sometimes you would like to alter it. There are those living upon the planet who have embodied with a compulsive, addictive nature. But this has been the gift to clear and to cleanse much within the soul itself. Many have chosen this path for its quick and fast results. Do you not see, Dear ones, what an honor it is, to have this personality that has courageously stepped forward to say "I see much within my Spirit which needs clarity, so I will work with greater force, with greater strength, with greater sense of purpose." It has been said that a weak person asks for assistance; this is not so. It is a very strong person who steps forward to say "Help me, assist me, come to me and give me your gift of grace. Understand me, be with me, and listen to me." This is indeed a person who has recognized a need, a need to clarify and to become stronger.

So you see, Dear ones, there is a great joy in the personality. It has been brought forth to offer much to the Spirit. We each have chosen a personality which fits handsomely with the desires of Spirit. It coats the Spirit and enables it to move throughout the world of matter. And it becomes a gift, a personal path. This great collective force in the universe has stepped forth to cloak your body with a teacher. This great teacher, the personality, has come to give you much. Welcome it! Touch it! And give thanks to it! For it has come from the center of Creation, the center of Creation that serves the mighty I AM Presence, the call to the universe, carried upon the wings of the Angelic Host.

Be thankful for trials and tribulations, for you are loved for your purpose. Life is purposeful. Life is the energy force of the ONE and its directive nature is one that flows. Say to yourself each day, "I AM thankful, I AM joyous, I AM gifted, I welcome my teacher, I welcome the gifts it brings to my Spirit. I AM thirsty for the universe to become ONE with me and I drink of the waters of knowledge from this fine teacher. I flow with the experience of this fine teacher and my Spirit is strengthened." Do you see, Dear ones, your Spirit is strengthened, strengthened with the universal principles of Forgiveness, of Compassion, of Grace, and of Love, for these are the attributes of the soul.

I call to the collective awakening of the planet at this time. I call within the inner core. I call to the personalities of the planet at this time. I call deep within and ask for the teacher to step forward. I AM lovingly yours, Sananda.

9

*We must learn how to feel. This is the heart, the energy
of love, and introduces us to the Fourth Dimension
and the group mind of ONE.*

Collective Cooperation
Saint Germain

Since moving the I AM America office several months ago, we have already gone through my inventory of I AM America Maps—about four hundred of them! Unfortunately the extra inventory is currently held in storage at Dan's parents' home. Sherry insists that I circumvent Dan altogether and call his father to make arrangements to get them. Early one morning, Sherry shows up at my door, "Well, we're out of Maps, and I have orders to fill." She points at her car, parked and still running in my driveway, "Hop in, we're picking 'em up."

I'm a bit pensive, but decide it is probably best to call Dan's father first. We chat for a few minutes and I can tell he's glad to hear my voice. "Yes, come on over," he says. "After all, they belong to you."

I'm relieved as we drive across the state border, heading to Lewiston. "You know, you should have had them all along," says Sherry, a bit annoyed.

"I know, I know," I answer. I've made one excuse after the other, purposely avoiding this inevitable ending.

Dan's father opens the door with a smile and gives me a hug. "Well, they're all here."

We move at least a dozen large packages of unrolled Maps and when the last package is loaded into the back of Sherry's station wagon, he stands for a moment in silence and then with a sober tone in his voice, says, "I don't understand all of this about my son. First he divorces Jane. Then he moves and wants to change his job. Then he meets you and the two of you move in with each other. Now he is with Carrie. I can't keep it all straight." His values harken from a different generation; once you're married, you stay married. You keep your promises.

In spite of my initial indecision, I feel a forward step of independence as we drive back across the bridge toward Asotin.

"You know, Dan was very abusive to you," says Sherry.

Before Asotin, Sherry lived in the wilderness of Alaska. It was there that she had become a certified counselor and had helped many women out of abusive relationships. "Let's unload these Maps, and then take a look at the cards," she says as we pull into the driveway.

One of the first tarot cards she turns up is the Devil. She hands me the card. "Take a good, long look."

I hold the card of shadows which depicts the Prince of Darkness, the destructive beast, Beelzebub, angel of the bottomless pit—and two distraught figures, a man and a woman are both hopelessly chained to him. "So is this about facing my dark side?" I ask.

"Yes," says Sherry, "but it's a little more than that. This is also a card of addiction and you are addicted to bad relationships. Because of your co-dependence, you're afraid to cut this destructive chain."

As she turns over the next few cards, their pattern accurately weaves many current themes of my life. It's a story that I've been intimately familiar since my separation from Dan almost three months ago. And Sherry's advice clearly echoes the same issues Paul pointed out to me about a month ago.

Three cards with the suit of swords symbolize my need for personal empowerment, and then the Queen of Wands appears—suggesting that I can obtain the necessary strength and independence needed for my healing journey. I sigh, "I know it intellectually . . . but, I don't feel it."

"You still love him, don't you?" says Sherry.

"Of course I do—but it's over." I hesitate for a minute, "Will I ever find love again?"

Immediately Sherry gathers the cards on the kitchen table, shuffles them, and lays out three new cards. "Oh," she gasps, "this is powerful . . . three major cards: the Hermit, the Emperor, and the Empress.

"There is someone coming, soon. But he is still hidden from you until you complete your own inner work." She continues, "But you will recognize him immediately. He is a teacher, in fact, a powerful, talented teacher. And in the end, well, this person will be the big love of your life." Sherry points to the Empress, an archetype of feminine power, glowing in the self-realization of inner strength, intuition, and wisdom—everything that, at this particular moment, I am not feeling.

As I turn the key to open my front door, I hear someone leaving a message on my answering machine—it's Dan. My heart pounds and I nervously rush to grab the receiver.

"Oh, Lori, was just leaving you a message . . . heard from my dad that you picked up the Maps."

"Yeah, sorry I didn't have time to let you know . . ." I'm a little out of breath and try to keep my composure.

"Are you going to be around today?" he asks. "I have another packet of Maps, and thought I'd drop them off."

"Ummm . . . yeah, that would be fine." As I hang up, I notice that my skin is flushed. I close my eyes and visualize the golden Empress, surrounded with poise and self-confidence.

"Well this will be a nice cabin for you and the kids for the summer," Dan remarks when he arrives. I've just given him the nickel tour of my little home. "Say, I was wondering if you'd let Carson spend the weekend with John? I'm taking the kids camping; I think they'll have a fun time together."

Our sons, close in age to one another, always enjoyed each other's company, but something doesn't feel right. "Let me think about it."

Dan moves closer and reaches for me. I take a step back and then calmly state, "You know, I'm seeing someone."

He flinches. "Oh . . ." There's disappointment on his face, "I'm happy for you." And then after a long silence, "Maybe this will be *the one* for you."

After another painful silence I purposely glance at my watch, "Thanks for bringing over the Maps, and I'll get back with you about the camping trip."

As he drives off, I think about the invitation; he wants some sort of a relationship with me, but I'm not certain we could ever be friends . . . and mid-thought, something grabs ahold of me—just like the young woman chained to an unknown tyrant.

That evening, I call Dan and say yes to the camping trip. Of course I justify my decision: it's summer, and the boys will have fun. Plus, it's time I grow up, accept that our relationship has changed, and act like an adult.

It is odd after a love affair ends. Even though you know for a fact that it is over—in this case, run-over, dead, squashed, completely irretrievable and unresuscitatable— yet I'm haunted by its Spirit of unknown possibility.

I swear that the ghost of unrequited love overcomes me as I walk down the grocery aisle with my son. We are picking out treats for him to take for the weekend and I see the bright tin of animal crackers, which I know is one of Dan's favorites. Like a possessed woman, I place it in the grocery cart.

When Dan arrives, I help Carson with his sleeping bag and hand him the tin. "Make sure you give these to Dan." Am I crazy? I think as I watch Dan ride off with my son and my romantic notions secretly embedded in the tin of animal crackers.

The girls and I have a quiet, yet active weekend. We pack a picnic and lay our suntanned, oily bodies on the white sand at the river's edge. They giggle and splash and I sunbathe and fantasize about the boys' camping trip and how much Dan will yearn for me around the lonely campfire.

The boys return exactly on time, late Sunday afternoon. I can tell that Carson is a bit sad that the trip is over, but happy to be home. He settles in with the girls in front of the television, and I walk out with Dan to his pick-up and ask, "How was the trip?"

"Oh, they had a good time," he replies, a little matter-of-fact. "Well, thanks again," he says and almost peels out of the driveway.

An hour later I ask Carson if he had a good time and question him about what they did and if he learned anything new. Carson is quiet and then thoughtfully responds, "I really had fun learning how to sharpen knives and throw them."

"What! Who showed you how to throw knives?" I would never allow him to touch a knife, let alone throw one.

"The girl with Dan," says Carson. "Carrie."

My heart drops into my stomach. Then I remember the tin of animal crackers . . . I had actually thought that he missed me!

And then I really think about it: Why the suggestible move toward me? And why did he invite my son, whom he knew would inevitably tell me? Sherry was right; Dan was abusive and not only had I been willfully blind, but I was enabling this behavior.

I call him immediately. "Dan, I am very angry at you. Why didn't you tell me that Carrie was going on the camping trip?"

He is nonchalant, "Well, I thought you knew. You've known all along that she and I are in a relationship."

I take a deep breath. "I can't be your friend. We need a break." I hang up.

The next evening before our session, I fill Sherry in on all of the details. "I told you, kid," she says, "and you keep running back for more."

"Yes, I guess so . . . I wonder what the Masters would say about all of this." Sherry just nods; by now she knows they'd have plenty to say.

The following selection is jammed-packed with progressive viewpoints on love, how to set boundaries that encourage spiritual growth and overcome our genetic patterns of ego-based survival instinct. These acts are based on self-honesty and ultimately our surrender to love—real love.

According to the Spiritual Teachers, the Earth is a unique planetary setting for souls to fully develop the Heart Chakra, and this precedes a vital leap into Fourth Dimensional experience. This is the evolutionary crux: as our spiritual development progresses into the ever-important experience of feeling, it is through this initiatory familiarity that our consciousness is then prepared to experience the ONE.

This spiritual understanding is essential to grasp in order to fully comprehend the Earth's current susceptibility and vulnerability to worldwide catastrophe—Earth

Changes. The Spiritual Teachers vow that certain changes are indeed necessary so we can all change collectively. They claim, "It is not a matter of survival, it is a matter of being." Being is analogous to feeling, spiritually awakened, and experiencing.

This lesson leads to provocative questions about our future governments and the existence of the one percent, and how we—the seemingly futile ninety-nine percent—can restructure and live with healing and joy before, during, and after the great changes. Saint Germain prophesies, and I'm paraphrasing, "Walls will break down as man starts to understand the love vibration which beats in all hearts."

Sherry insists that this is, "A tall order."

Indeed, it is. But at this point, my pursuits will no longer entertain becoming *the one* for any singular, earthly man. In order to spiritually grow and evolve, I now aspire to embrace a nonpossessive, all-inclusive ONE.

⌇

Greetings, Beloveds, I AM Saint Germain. I will act tonight as facilitator for this question and answer period. This evening I come to you, I come to you to work with that of the Christ Energy. I have not brought others with me this evening, as I have felt directed to come to you with my energy and radiance. And so, direct your questions to me, for I AM here to help and assist you and I AM honored to do this work with you. As in all similar discourses, I ask your permission to participate with you. Do I have your approval?

Response: "Yes."

I AM here to educate you tonight on that of the heart energy of the Earth at this time, that which is the functioning Heart Chakra of the planet, that which is of the love vibration. For you see, there is much out upon the planet at this time, many differing paths, many truths, many ways of discerning the enormous deluge of information which exists upon the planet. It is of vast importance that we impress to you, Dear ones, that the work of the heart, the love energy, is the common thread and the common goal. For you see, Dear ones, the love energy and the love vibration is the total resonance of this planet. You see her position in the planetary system at this time. Those who come to embody on the planet have come to learn to feel, to feel this energy in its highest vibration. Do you understand?

Response: "Yes."

It is a great honor to be brought to this schoolroom to be taught to feel. There are many other planets that you also learn and go to, to gain your lessons of Mastery. There are those where you Master technical and knowledge fields that are associated with the mental plane. There are other planets where you go to learn and to Master physicalness, survival, and basic evolution. However, those who come to this planet at this time have a step in their evolution, that which is the fourth step. The fourth step is understanding the love vibration, understanding the Fourth Dimension, that which is the functioning Heart Chakra Center, the common thread of all becoming ONE. For you see, Dear ones, you all start as ONE and differentiate in your embodiments, working through that which is the physicalness of your nature and the mental capabilities. Then you are raised to this point, the Fourth Dimension, or the love vibration. This brings you to ONE, with boundaries and without boundaries.

You have learned much of boundaries through your evolutionary state. This is what we call the genetic memory, the genetic coding, which is associated with the DNA, that which is separate from Cellular Awakening. The love vibration is that which is closely associated with that of the Cellular Awakening. For you see, Dear ones, this is the vibration with which this force works.

There is much misinformation out about setting boundaries. We have learned to set boundaries through that which is the ego state, that which was developed for your survival in physical and mental planes. And now, you must learn that the next process is to set this Veil down, the shedding of the curtain, or the shredding of the curtain. You must see that this curtain is being torn for you to understand and to touch this realm of Fourth Dimension. You are to learn to feel and, through the feeling, there is the one commonality, the one vibration which merges one energy vibration to the next. And that is love. My Dear hearts, do you have questions regarding this discourse?

Question: "We had to go through feelings of pain?"

We are speaking here of learning the responsibility of action and motion and motive. We are speaking of learning to feel, learning to feel through these many, many experiences that you have in the physical and mental realms, so that you are open for that of the spiritual. So, you move through the motions of pain, pain associated with a given experience. Perhaps someone has stolen from you or taken something from you. And so you move through this, judging your Brother, hating your Brother, or feeling disharmony towards another of your Brothers. And so you are able to sense a state of separation. And through this state of separation, you experience discomfort. Through this discomfort, you are moved to that of commonality, the thread. You come to a point of hopelessness, helplessness. Where do I go from here? This is the point of Cellular Awakening. For you are driven and directed. Your cells spin in such a way that there is no other way for them to go. Do you understand?

Question: "Yes. Sort of like hitting bottom, so that you can take a good look at where you are?"

This is an honest evaluation of where we are. Of course, honesty is a concept which varies from individual to individual, as you are well aware of in human embodiment.

Question: "Yes. I would like to ask if it's too late to change the Earth destruction? Will it still go on if everyone learns love and feeling for each other?"

Perhaps what we should speak about is not love within itself, but surrender, surrender to a force that is this love force. Many are learning through what you would call the hard knocks, to surrender to this force. However, we, at this time, have brought this message of great hope and light and love to mankind, so that this should not happen. There are things that are timeless and ageless and the Prophets have spoken long about Earth Change at this point of millennium, preceding one age into another. So you see, we speak of the Cellular Awakening and what leads one to come to this point of Cellular Awakening. It is the dropping of the cells, that of the genetic. And you must see this as well within any transitional state, as you move from Third Dimension to Fourth Dimension.

You must welcome this time, that which you see as cataclysm, that which you see as a hard time, a depression, a time of great need. It is also a time of great hope, it is a time of great awakening, it is a time to rejoice. For you see, we have said, "before you, the feast is prepared" and we ask for you to come and sup with us, to partake of this great time, for you see, it is a monumental leap. There are indeed Earth Changes which will occur that cannot be stopped. But there are also those that can and those that you must see in terms of your energy vibration, how we affect one another, how we meld with one another, how we become ONE energy. This is the point, the focus of Earth Change information. It is for people to unite and to see themselves as ONE with Divine Purpose, ONE as a cooperative unit, ONE who must work together to seek active solutions to the problems we have, active solutions in the dancing of the Flame, this great joy, this great thing called life.

Question: "So, in other words, by giving us all a disaster that we can't deal with alone, we are forced to draw together and work together and love together, in order to survive? Is that the way it works?"

I would like to address your question, however, it is not a matter of survival, it is a matter of being. There will be many who will leave embodiment during this time and yet their energy force will still be felt upon the planet. For you see, even as you leave embodiment, you leave the resonance of your etheric levels. This too must be adjusted, to cooperate with the new life force that is undertaking this great birth and awakening upon this planet. Have I answered your question?

Question: "Yes. I don't understand exactly, when the cells change along with the Earth Changes, will we still have physical bodies?"

Some will be in physical embodiment but the majority will have a physical embodiment that is altered and different or changed from that which you have your shell about you now. Please understand, there will be many who will be discarding the body during this time, not through death, but through that of the Ascension and taking on the new robe, the seamless cloak, as we have called. The seamless garment is comprised of higher etheric elements. For you see, in the physical we have the density, the density of matter vibrating against matter. And so we remove the matter and what is there to vibrate? That which is the spiritual essence also vibrates and moves through its Cellular Awakening and you are able to see an actual physical form which comes forth from that ONE which dances with the light of beauty.

And so, we have those who are leaving the actual physical embodiment, through the transition called death. Some of them will be altered in their state in the higher etheric realms and brought back to this planet to continue their growth and development, to work in cooperative harmony with the other beings of light who will be embodied at this time. There are those who will not be allowed to return to the planet until they have gone through other steps of mental development and also survival mode therapies of understanding their genetic coding. For you see, Dear ones, it is not a matter of less or more, or right or wrong. It is a matter of what is attracted to the Vibration of the Planet and those who leave will be those who will be attracted to the Vibration of other Solar Systems. And there are those who shall return, through their attraction and vibration to this planet. There are also those who will never leave through the transition of death but will simply step forward and go forth into this garment, this which has been manifested through the Higher Self, through the Mastery of the love vibration.

Question: "Is there any way to know at this point, which way we will be going? Is there any way that we can tell how we are going to react?"

We have spoken about the ability to feel, the ability to intuit, the ability to feel one's radiance. You have also learned much about what is called the Human Aura or the light field. There are those that you feel harmonious with. There are those who have mastered the elements of cooperation. This is how you will be able to tell those who are able to move into a collective group and also produce a harmonious effect from their collective effort. Do you understand? Do you see how governments upon the planet work, at times, to not produce a harmonious end result? And yet, there are those who work together, who do. Only those who are able to produce a cooperative, collective, harmonious effect will be staying. However, you are saying, is there a way that we may tell how a person may stay or person will go during this time? It is largely up to the freewill of the individual. However, you will be able to sense and to know through that which surrounds him. You will see the fruit that comes from the tree in his garden and you will be able to see and know a person by their work.

Question: "Speaking about our government, how much longer will it be the way it is?"

There will be several years of chaos after the major Earth Changes begin and the government will try to collect itself and come in. At that time, a global scale government will be organized and they too shall attempt to come in and to alleviate some of the disorganization. However, it will be largely left up to man, again, to reorganize and to function at the government level. But this time, we will look deeply within our hearts for the way that we organize and become ONE with this planet and ONE with ourselves.

Question: "Will our government ever address any of the pollution?"

Not with the current structure that you are functioning under. This is part of the reason for what you would term, "cataclysmic Earth Change," for there will have to be some major movements of land and major movement of collective consciousness in order for governments to truly address the needs, hopes, wishes, and dreams of the hearts of man.

Question: "Did the Native Indians have the proper way to live on the Earth and is that the way of our future, back to the earth, tepees, and nomads, living off roots, fish, and berries?"

There will be a transitional period where this will be of importance for survival of the physical. However, it is through the heart of man, that which lifts him to the Ascended Master energy, which you will come to understand as Fourth Dimension. All needs and wants will be met. It is our hope to impart technologies at this time which will raise the vibrations of man and also raise one to a vision of a Golden Age.

In this millennium time, that which has come knocking at the door at this time, there is much reorganization and restructuring to be done. There is much work to be done. There is also, at this time, a great need and a great call for the technologies to come forth. There is also a great need and a great call for man to not slip back into this more primal way of living during the transition but to hold the vision, that through this period of time will become a new way of living, a new life, a new garden. For you see, man was brought to this planet to learn and now man is brought to this planet to restructure and to live in joy. This period of time of joy is a gift. This is a time of rest, a time of solitude, and a time to experience, in the learning capacity, as one would look at Earth as a great schoolroom, a place for re-creation.

Question: "In other words, there will be a time where we struggle to survive, so to speak, and then, the changes will bring such new bodies and such a New Earth that we won't have to struggle to live, it will be a joy to live?"

It will be a joy to live, with all barriers and walls broken down, as man starts to understand the love vibration which beats within all hearts. He will give freely of himself to his Brother and his Brother will give freely of himself back. Do you understand?

Question: "Yes. What about people who prey on others and look for people who give, will they be gone?"

There are two things which must happen to this type of energy force. Their vibration must be raised through the collective consciousness or through the technologies which will be imparted. Or they will simply become attracted to another Solar System or schoolroom, so that they are able to become who they are.

Question: "Will we be separated according to our Auras, so that we can live in harmony?"

Specifically, through the heart.

Question: "There is no way that people can live in harmony unless everyone's consciousness is raised to a level that is compatible, is that correct?"

This is correct. We are working with, what is called, collective cooperative energy and many will feel the need to move into community and we encourage this at this time, so that people begin to learn and understand how we all work together in a synergistic way. Each will complement the other and yet, recognize each for the individual talent or individual gift that they have brought into embodiment. It is of most importance that we learn cooperation.

Question: "The last time the Earth did a polar shift, if people were not raised in vibration, did they revert back to living off the land and struggling for survival?"

There was a chance that they would have moved into what is called the Fourth Dimension reality. For you must understand, in the crucial period of transition, there is a point where you hit what is called the ninety-nine percentile. At this point, it takes a collective force working together and ninety-nine percent must be prepared and ready to do this. If this percentile is affected by the one percent, we experience that which is the cataclysmic changes.

Response: "That's a big order, ninety-nine percent. What is the percentage now?"

To be specific, it is fifty-eight percent.

Question: "Could you tell us what we can expect locally?"

You are experiencing what is called a thermal cooling and you will experience a more temperate climate during your spring and summer seasons. However, in your winters, you will notice that they will not be as cold and will become dryer. What you are moving towards is a more consistent climate within your energy area.

Question: "Warmer and more of the same all the time?"

This is precise.

Question: "No seasons? How about the winds, will there be more winds, heavy bad winds?"

Of course wind is always that which relies upon the collective consciousness, that which lies approximately 240 kilometers away from you. To measure your wind, look within that distance around you and read the collective consciousness from that area and you will get an idea of the wind patterns that will impart upon your area.

Question: "The wind is brought on by what, anger?"

The wind is brought on upon that which is not working in the cooperative force, that which you call, as scattered.

Question: "Scattered energies cause wind?"

This is precise.

Question: "So, from this circle around us, the energy of the people help create the weather?"

This is precise.

Question: "Is our physical home going to have to be abandoned because of water?"

I am not allowed to impart this knowledge to you at this time, for you see, we are dealing with the collective consciousness. As I have said to you, we are asking for ninety-nine percent. You call that a tall order, however, it is a crucial order, for there are other Solar Systems which are relying upon this act of the shift into Fourth Dimension consciousness upon the Earth. And this is the seventh time she has been given this opportunity.

Question: "Then why do I feel like we're ants being farmed by superior intelligence at times, are we?"

My Dear, you are an individual and you are loved and blessed. You are created in God's image, you are no ant. You are a Child of God and remember that above all things.

Question: "I've read a lot about people that you call astronauts or space beings. There are a number of books out about space beings harvesting people that are ready to be harvested and be moved. Are they speaking of those who are being drawn to other planets?"

This is true at this time, for within what is called the genetic awakening, they are being drawn to where they must go and be at that time.

Question: "These people are actually lifted in space ships? Or is this just a form that people can understand?"

It is a great crime that your governments have allowed the influence of other Solar Systems of the dualistic nature within your plane at this time. However, through their agreements that they have formed, there have been others that have taken on physical embodiment, who come from those Solar Systems. And yes, there will be those who will leave through that method and those who will go to those systems at that time. However, I would suggest that you stay if you feel directed to stay, to learn that of Fourth Dimensional reality, for this is a grand opportunity for those who are here at this schoolroom at this time, to experience this period. For you see, this is a cycle, one which has occurred six other times and this is the seventh offering.

Question: "Well, I really want to stay and observe and help. I want to learn and I feel very drawn to this work. I do have a fear that I don't want anything to happen to me so I'll miss it."

My beloved Sister, we love you and thank you for your desire to serve. This is the Cellular Awakening for those who are dedicated to service, those who are dedicated to Oneness, those who want to move beyond the self into selfless Selfhood.

Response: "I feel it is most important that laws are changed and that the focus of government is changed to a point where there is love and honor and protection of people's rights and the Earth's rights. And I want to be here to see it changed."

My Dear, I would like to remind you that this is assured. However, as we have spoken of the ninety-nine percentile, there is that one percent chance that it could not occur.

Question: "In other words, if there isn't ninety-nine percent, none of these things, the New Age will not happen?"

No, my Dear, what I speak of is the one-percent chance that the collective consciousness will not allow this to occur.

Question: "So, in other words, we have to work to make it happen?"

That is correct. It is self-conscious correction. It is the path of walking what you believe to be truth, to exercise your truths, and to work together in a cooperative way to bring these truths into a synergistic motion.

10

*Change is engendered in mind, and ultimately transformation
of self is determined through the habits of thought.*

Emergence

Saint Germain
Mary
Kuan Yin
Soltec

I'm still in a bit of an emotional whirlwind so to keep my mind straight, I set my alarm for 5:30 a.m. every morning and start the day with a brisk bicycle ride along the river. Her waters appear still and peaceful, yet inside I'm still stirring with so many unsettled thoughts. David is a calm and reassuring influence, but unfortunately he lives in San Francisco. So, I'm a bit unsure just where our friendship is headed.

As aggravated and disappointed I am with Dan, I still miss him. I've adapted to working with Sherry, but I do miss having a partner, both spiritually and personally. Sherry's last tarot reading echoes in my mind, "You need to do your inner work, first." I am now aware of my self-created Sword of Damocles, and I've realized it's better not to expect so much from myself and to take it easy. I've also come to the conclusion that if the Spiritual Teachers really want me to work again with a spiritual partner, that they will make appropriate arrangements. For now, I must focus on my work and genuinely exercise faith.

The trance sessions with Sherry, Lynne, and Glenda are undoubtedly a godsend. I'll often walk into Sherry's living room to find Steve sitting in his bathrobe, holding a glass of milk. I tease him as I sit down at the kitchen table, "Hitting the hard stuff again?" Steve chuckles, turns off the television and quietly vanishes, or should I say, *escapes* to the bedroom. I sometimes wonder if our sessions are a bit of a stretch for him, considering that he is agnostic. Sherry telepathically senses my concerns and reassures me, "Everything is just fine with Steve . . . and just so you know, if he had a problem, he'd let us know."

She has a prepared a lengthy list of questions, and I ask, "Are you sure we'll get answers for them all?"

"You may not know this," she replies, "but I rarely ask any of these questions. They usually answer them before I get to them—I just check off the question."

"Do you think they can see them, and are saving you the trouble?"

"Well, that might be one way to understand the phenomenon. But I think there may be more to this. I think we have formed a group mind, and that group mind anticipates our needs and is simply responding."

This idea is thought-provoking. "You mean these sessions may be responding to our collective energy and our preconceived thoughts and beliefs?"

Sherry is to the point. "Exactly."

We settle into a quiet space, and group mind or not, soon the words of the Spiritual Teachers fill the room.

In this lesson the four Spiritual Teachers—Saint Germain, Mary, Kuan Yin, and Soltec—form a collective consciousness with their energies. I think that this lesson is inherently personal, and designed to give me encouragement during this difficult juncture. Yet, this invaluable message of change is also an important universal teaching.

This selection reminds us that we can change many things: our diet, exercise, and personal habits. But the most important change is indeed the change within. And change is engendered in our mind, dictated through the habits of our thoughts. This lesson also continues invaluable teachings on the Cellular Awakening, the Blue Flame of Protection, and the Mighty Tube of Light.

Sherry sneaks in a few unanswered questions for the everyday person about the biblical Christ and anti-Christ. This inevitably leads the Spiritual Teachers to disclose their expanded awareness about our world government, planetary shift, parallel universes and dimensions, and ultimately Earth Change. Finally the lesson ends with a reminder that the real preparation for the New Times is to, "Collect your mind. Collect your being."

Welcome, I AM Saint Germain. This evening, I would like to introduce those around me, those who come to assist in your awakening. As you are well familiar with my work and who I AM, there are those who have come to also assist in our discourse this evening. May I introduce to you, Beloved Mary, Beloved Kuan Yin, my Brother Soltec, and my Brother Sananda? We are forming a collective unit this evening to give you our collective energy and are here for your assistance. And as you have understood from past evenings of discourse, we need your permission to continue this work. Do we have your permission, Dear ones?

Response: "Yes."

I AM most willing to assist you this evening and open the floor for questions.

Question: "I'd like to ask if there is anything that we should do to help Lori keep her energy up while she's channeling and would you scan her body to see that she doesn't get too tired? Is there something she should be doing during the day to be a better channel?"

Of course, we have spoken to her about the need to enhance the diet. And also about the air you breathe and the water that you take in. There is also a need to take in a higher density of chlorophyll-based foodstuffs into the system, that which contains the molecular level of 2.8% chlorophyll to that of hydrogen and oxygen into the system. There is also a great need for use of the Violet Flame. That is, the affirmation and meditation, which assists the Cellular Awakening, that which we have spoken about in similar discourses.

It is not so much our concern over diet, as over habits, habits associated with the mind and the thinking, as well as habits associated with the will and understanding of the will, as turned over to the God Source. There are also habits which affect the physiology, associated with the consumption of animal products, specifically, that of lactose and also that which contains high synthetic sugar content. It is important at this time, that your metabolic rate is kept at a slower rate, for as the Cellular Awakening occurs, you have an increased metabolism. It is important to not be taking in those substances that come through artificial means but only those that come from the highest natural state. Those that come from the planet itself are offered up to assist mankind through the Cellular Awakening. When the metabolic rate is increased in the physiology, so is the spinning of the cells around the axis center of the eight-sided crystalline structure. Do you understand?

Response: "Yes. Is there any way to stop smoking when we have trouble doing that?"

In terms of ingestion, beta-carotene, or what you have known as high dosages of vitamin A into the system, assists the bloodstream in cleansing. Also, a high intake of pure water would be of great benefit. Of course, as we have always stated, the Violet Flame gives the highest degree of assistance. Are you familiar with the Violet Flame and its use upon the planet?

Question: "How do we call upon the Violet Flame? How do we bring it to us? Or use it?"

The Violet Flame is the highest principle that you may use during this time. It is the principle of transformation, that which you call through your Higher Self and your Higher Self contacts that of the universal Source. It is the Flame of Mercy and Forgiveness, that which is extended to others, as well as to yourself. You may call through affirmation, as I have stated:

I AM A BEING OF VIOLET FIRE. I AM THE PURITY GOD DESIRES.

Or, you may call upon through your meditation, through the visualization of the Violet Flame, starting at the base of the feet, coming up and surrounding the body, enveloping it in an egg-like shape. The Violet Flame is then encircled with the white pure light, that which is known as the Tube of Light. Around this Tube of Light, call upon the Blue Flame, the Blue Flame for protection of truth, so that which you call upon is ever protected and ever sustained. There are two concepts concerning Violet Flame usage. There are those that insist that its use be no less than nine times a day. There are others that call upon it once in the lifetime and keep it sustained around them at all times. However, I have found for myself and in my embodiment, that my use of it no less than twelve times a day assisted me greatly. However, it depends upon the person that is using it and of course you know about freewill. Have I answered your question?

Response: "Yes. I'd like to now ask about the Anti-Christ that we've read about in the Bible. Is there such a person and who is it? What is the purpose of the Anti-Christ?"

Yes, my Child, there is such a person, a person who is acting with a collective force, a collective force which serves its part in awakening the children of the planet. For you see, these collective energies, as they are placed in your path, are there for you to be tested. They come to you so you may learn the art of discernment. Yes, there is this being and this entity draws from a collective energy source.

Question: "What will he do? Does he work with our government?"

This is a being who contains within it thirty soul entities, which have at this time, turned their face from the light. However, it is our hope that at one time, they shall return from the source from which they came.

Question: "Does he work with our world government? "

Of course he does. And I am not permitted to disclose any more information regarding such. For you see, Dear ones, there is that information that we are permitted to disclose to you and there is that which we guard. Do you understand?

Question: "In other words, it wouldn't be a test if we knew all the answers?"

This is precise. For you see, as you have come to understand, there is neither good nor bad, there is neither light nor dark. But there is freedom and the individual path to choose. And to give you this information at this time would confuse your right to choose and interfere with your individual freedoms. Do you understand?

Question: "Yes. Is the government aware of the coming Earth Changes? If so, do they plan to tell the people?"

The coming Earth Changes are arbitrary, as I have always stated. They are projected into the future, a future time which is predestined or predated from a moment in time. You must understand, that as you project into the future, you are projecting into the conditions at a given moment and conditions change from day to day. Perhaps you project yourself into a rainstorm. You look out the window and you see the rain falling and so you walk into the storm and feel the droplets on your face and see the clouds about you. Yet again, if you look through the window and you see it is a clear day, you walk out, feeling the sun beating upon your face. Do you understand that this is much how the concept of time travel works? You find the portal, the door, you look through it and then you walk through it. Do you see how this is changed and variable from day to day? For the force that you work with is not a force which stays constant. It is a force that changes in a Co-creative way, changing each day, changing from its limitation. Do you understand?

Response: "Yes."

And so, each day is different. Each day is changed. That which we call the upcoming Earth Changes has been preordained through the collective consciousness of mankind for two thousand years. And so, there are the changes which are inevitable, which must come. I can assure you, one is the removal of separation. I can assure you, there will be the movement of Third to Fourth Dimensional consciousness. Also, I can assure you is the healing of the human body and transfiguration. For you see, this is the process of Ascension, you rising to ONE with your Higher Self. This happens through many layers, through mental layers and emotional layers, also that which you have known as etheric or astral layers. However, the direct approach is to call to your mighty I AM Presence and ask for the direct link, the direct Cellular Awakening, which happens as a direct course of being.

Question: "I would like to ask Soltec about the Mayan Calendar and how that is connected to me at this time?"

Saint Germain is calling him forward.

Welcome, beloved Sister, I AM Soltec. You have questions regarding the calendar which has been brought forth through the Council of Nine or the Nine Seen?

Question: "I'm getting a lot of reading stuff; several different books have been falling into my lap, particularly having to do with the year 2012 and the working out of the mathematical formulas for the alignment or realignment of the axis."

He is going over to a blackboard and writing a series of numbers.

Question: "Can you tell us what this means?"

My Dear Sister, this is a formula upon which much of the data has been based. This is a molecular, mathematical formula associated with the structure of time and days, Earth units as you have known them. This is based upon a principle of nines, that which is the three times three.

Question: "Why is it important that I come forth with this information right now? How can I help people with this?"

It is important to understand that one cycle leads to the next, that as one cycle begins to close, another opens. We are not seeing the end of one cycle, without seeing the emergence of a new one built upon the next. It is important that much hope is given to people during this time. It is important that people keep clarity of vision. It is also important that people have the technology to assist them during this Time of Awakening. And also, it is important that this technology is dispensed into the hands of humanity. Dear Sister, work with this formula and reveal its secrets to the many that you will find. I AM here for your assistance and will be glad to assist you on this project. May I help you more?

Question: "Was there something in this workshop that we're putting together that I should be aware of? I'm not sure who this information is for at this point, I guess that's my question."

There will be those who will be led to this information through you. It has been given to you and now you have the thought matrix to attract to you that which will unlock the keys.

Response: "I'll receive the information then when I need it and am willing to work further with it. Right at this moment, it would be helpful to me if you would strengthen my memory of earlier times when I worked with these mathematical figures."

He's showing me something else too. He has a metal cone device. It's like a funnel and he is blowing through it. He is sending a current of air through it and the way that the current runs explains some of these cycles, how they work and interact. The airs goes in a spiral through the funnel and then off on the spirals are also other circles or currents of air that twist around the spiral. He's taking it apart and showing it to me. It has a kind of ribbing in it and there is also a series of circles. The air currents go through sort of a little series of gates.

The calendar and the air patterns of the Earth are related in time. What we are explaining to you are parallels, parallels that exist not only in weather patterns but also in time. They are closely associated and the parallels in weather have been given to man so they may understand, at the simplest levels, those of the parallel dimensions, those that you have explored as parallel universes. This is a concept hard for man to perceive, as he embodies into one dense universe, that which is his one reality. However, there are many realities that coexist with man. even in his current embodiment.

At any given time, a man or woman in an embodiment may have up to fifteen embodiments existing in parallel dimensions of time upon the planet. However, we would like to assure you that with each embodiment, or parallel embodiment, you stay or embody upon that planet. You do not exist, at this time, on other planets. You choose one Solar System to send your vibration or frequency to and you embody among the many dimensions, up to fifteen.

And so this Mayan Calendar that you speak of, is also the timing of one dimension merging to the next, that point of the gate, when the gate opens or the gate closes. You have gone through a cycle of the gate closed and now, the gate begins to open again. One dimension or parallel dimension, as we speak of, becomes ready to touch that of another. It is that of the planetary glimpse, where you are able to perceive all dimensions at once and partake of all dimensions at once, before the gate closes again. It is a period of time known as Transition and also leads one into a period of time known as a Millennium. Do you understand?

Question: "Yes. Is there anything else that I need to know about at this time?"

It is important, my Dear Sister, for you to remain clear with your vision and your work. Remain clear with that which you feel is your Divine Purpose. As you receive this glimpse into the parallel universe, that which has been predicted and which you call the Nine Seen or the Mayan Calendar, coming from the three times three, it is important for you to remain clear so that you may see this glimpse.

Response: "Thank you."

Question: "I'd like to ask about hydroponics versus greenhouses. Are these things necessary for the next few years? Is the weather going to be so difficult that it will be hard to grow things?"

There will be major weather changes upon the planet as one goes through this planetary shift. It is very important that you also become aware of the many alternatives to growing foodstuffs. However, as we have discussed, there will be a lesser need for food upon the planet as one becomes aware of the higher body. Yet, there will be those who will still feel the need to serve the body and also replenish its nutrients. Hydroponics is indeed an intensive way to grow these foodstuffs and is a better way to obtain the foods which have a clearer density of nutrients into the system. There is also that which we have spoken of, the chlorophyll-based foods, those which assist in the Cellular Awakening and we also suggest the high use of these. In hydroponics, we are able to . . .

He's scanning.

place within the chemical solutions, that which you actually need, those elements, minerals, to produce the end result of which you would like to achieve.

He's looking at this greenhouse, comparing the two.

In weighing this situation, my Sister, I AM exploring that which you have termed as greenhouse. It is in my opinion the hydroponics would be the clearer way to achieve the goal.

Response: "Thank you. Was there any particular thing you would like to present to us?"

At this time, listen for sounds which allow the human body, through the Chakra Centers, to align to harmony, that which is known as the Cellular Awakening. There are tones which assist in this and there are products which also assist in this. We will also be working with the use of color and its vibration, also the use of light and different densities of light. Of course, you have worked much with prayer and affirmation. Also, use through the Throat Chakra, that which is affirmation, the use of word, for it has been said, "In the Beginning was the Word," and this is indeed powerful. However, the use of sound is used in more universal application, that which goes beyond the planet and extends off into the cosmos. Also, that sound within itself aligns one to the many universes which are in existence at this time, those universes of other dimensions within the Earth Plane and Planet at this time. I would be honored to assist in the formation of several products and ask if you would like to receive such.

Response: "Yes."

He's asking me if I'd like to channel this for you sometime. I will do that for you.

Question: "You talked a little bit about color and light. There is another here with us this evening and she's been working some with drawings and getting information about chakras and working with colors and color healing. Is that a good avenue for her to continue?"

The total integration of color, sound, and light is most pleasing and brings harmony to the body. It aligns the body and the Chakra Centers to the finer energies of the universe, those which are pulsating at a higher degree at this instant. For you see, Dear ones, the cosmic energies entering in at this time and all color and light which resonates with these energies are of vast importance, providing a perfect program for total integration and harmony for the Cellular Awakening.

Question: "She's been thinking about doing some color therapy. Is that appropriate for her to work on for this summer? "

It is most appropriate and we would gladly assist in such. We suggest working with hues of pink and densities of yellow and finding a sound harmonic that vibrates with them. Dear Sister, there is a contact for you to make in the city of Dallas, a center there for you to contact.

Question: "Could we ask now about the economy in the United States? And how we'll best be ready for what is coming?"

Saint Germain is coming forward.

You have asked the question about the economy and I will answer you most bluntly, Dear heart, that it is not stable at this time. We have spoken to you on previous occasions and have told you to go to your area, to collect your seeds, to collect your thoughts, to collect your being. We will continue our work upon the planet at this time. However, we have spoken of this period of Time of Transition and there are indeed tests, trials, and tribulations. It is our hope to never instill fear in your heart and to send our love and support at all times. We have spoken of the four pillars, the four pillars to shake.

Question: "Are the four pillars banks?"

Four families.

Question: "Is that the four families that run the country?"

It is indeed the four families and an introduction of a fifth family that is causing this.

Question: "Is it a power struggle?"

I'm sorry, they're leaving...

11

*The human aura breaks into seven distinct bodies of
light that drives human spiritual development.*

Seven Bodies

Saint Germain
Sananda
Hilarion

In order to understand the gist of the Cellular Awakening, Saint Germain shares this introduction to the human aura which forms a band of distinguishable layers of light, and each layer of light resonates or vibrates with a specific Chakra Center that can be separated into a "body of light." Each light body controls certain human functions, and in many ways drives human consciousness toward evolution and spiritual awakening. These definitions may help you to more clearly understand the Seven Bodies of Light.

First Light Body: The sexual urge, and as we evolve and grow through the lowest Chakra Center, our creative abilities awaken.

Second Light Body: A survival Chakra associated with instinct. This light body later evolves into our ability to sense and feel the Fourth Dimension.

Third Light Body: This center controls the basic human need to love another, and later evolves into our natural human need for community.

Fourth Light Body: An emotional body and as it develops through successive lifetimes drives the human experience beyond genetics into human spiritual evolution. This is the center of the Heart Chakra, and the "opening of the Heart."

Fifth Light Body: Another aspect of the emotional body, yet this light body controls the intellect and is also known as "The Mental Body."

Sixth Light Body: This important light body currently drives human evolutionary processes to develop and understand the Third Eye Chakra, and the ability to process information telepathically beyond the Third Dimension and into the Fourth

Dimension. According to the Spiritual Teachers this light body is the nexus for the beginning of the Cellular Awakening among humanity.

Seventh Light Body: This light body is often referred to by Saint Germain as a "gate," and it calibrates energy moving from the spiritual dimensions into the physical dimension. It serves as a pivotal point to regulate energies of both the Father Principle and the Mother Principle.

This lesson ends with fascinating information about star seeds and the current relationship of alien genetics to the different soul groups of humanity and their role in activating certain groups of people both toward Spiritual Awakening and interconnected portals of the Earth. Apparently our Chakra Centers are interconnected with the Vortices of Mother Earth.

∾

Saint Germain is present and around him are three angels, standing off to the side. Also with him is Sananda and another Ascended Being, whose name is Hilarion.

Welcome, my Beloved chela, I AM Saint Germain. I AM here for your assistance this day and realize the expediency of the work we do together, for during this Time of Transition, there is much to be covered. There are many loose ends still to be tied up, for as the consciousness shifts from Third to Fourth Dimension realities, there is much to be done within the Earth Plane. There is much work still to be done to harmonize the higher bodies of mankind. For you see, as the body de-densifies and takes on its new shell, we must align the electromagnetic currents of the other bodies. Let me explain this more thoroughly.

There are exactly seven layers which exist above the physical body. Each of these layers, corresponding to the energy points in the body, known as Chakras, must be aligned with the electromagnetic current of the planet. This too lines up to energy points within the Earth itself, for she too has seven layers, starting from the core and extending to the outer surface. And beyond this, there are again seven layers outside of the Earth surface, that which is known as the higher body of the Earth. And so you see, man is created much as she is herself. It is the combination of the two sparks, the Alpha and the Omega, the Mother and Father Principle, the Mother being that of the earth substance, the Earth Planet. Man, within his physical shell, contains this principle. And from the Father, the Logos, is the Spirit.

And so man has been created in both images, the Mother/Father Principle. Spirit comprises that which is in the higher realms, the spark of Divine Creation, the Mother Principle, that of the fertile ground, that which the Spirit has been planted upon.

And so we have seven layers, to seven more layers. Upon total integration and completion, one is ready for transfiguration or Ascension, as we call it. You enter into what is called Fifth Dimension reality, that which is the combined collective force of both layers, where one is able to move in and about through density and through Spirit at will. You, my Dear ones, my Dear Children are being prepared to move into the fourth reality, that which is the total alignment area. Fourth reality is that of harmony and cooperation, that which is learning to control these energies of the seven lower bodies and the seven higher bodies, to create with them, to understand and to attain At-ONE-ment with them, to prepare yourself for the next dimension, a dimension that is Mastery of such. Do you understand?

Question: "Yes. Are the seven bodies separate and do they each have a function of their own?"

There were times in First and Second and Third Dimension consciousness that the definition of such was more defined. The functions were broken into several parts, into more defined areas, as one would call it. And as you enter from this Third Dimensional reality into Fourth, it is important that they are defined for you to understand. Should we walk through these functions?

Response: "Yes, please."

We will start with the Mother Principle, that which is the fertile ground, that which is the nurturer that the Spirit is planted into. We speak of the lower energies, that of the lower bodies. This is the will to create. It is the creative energy, that which first surrounds and is ready to be impregnated with that of the higher principle, that is, the Divine Spark of Creation. The two work simultaneously together. It has been used as a sexual energy in the past, the need to reproduce. And in the higher form, from what is known as the "Logoic Principle." It is the will to create, these two functioning together.

The next body is understood as the will to survive. It is the survival instinct. It is that deep desire and need for life to continue. It is through this body that man has often fought his many wars. It is also from another principle, the need to nourish and to protect. From the Spirit, this comes forth as the need to continue life. We have the creation of life and the desire for life to continue. This comes from the next layer.

From the next body, we have the need to move to community, to work together as ONE. This is not through what is known as the love principle. This is the need for organisms of like to move together to like. It is that urge to be ONE with its Source, coming from what is known as the fourth body. The third body is known as the body to move to community and in the higher principle, if you were to visualize cells moving, first is the creative concept, then survival concept, then community concept. Do you understand?

Question: "Yes. Is this the same thing as the Chakras of the body?"

This is correct. And this information corresponds. We move to the next body. This is closely associated with the development of the emotions. The move to community develops the lower mental body. In higher Divine Principles, it is the structure and orderliness of Creation. As we move to this next principle, to this next body, we are discussing the development of the emotional body, that which is the need for a continuum. It is through the emotional body that life forms evolve, and are impressed. Up to this point, we have dealt with what is genetic memory. It is through the development of this next body, the emotional body, that one is prepared for what we have been discussing as Cellular Awakening.

Question: "Is this the Heart Chakra, the emotional body where the Spirit moves through?"

This is correct. It is also the point of impregnation from the Father Spirit, that which is anchored within. It is also the Source of the Spirit. This is the center from which it comes. We move up to the next body, which is the need for the extension of the emotional body with others who have developed their emotional body. You have known it as communication. It is the skills of like mind and like emotional body, meeting like mind and like emotional body. This principle goes beyond cooperation. It is linked still to that of the seeding process. It finer tunes that of the third body. They are linked closely together and bonded through what is known as the emotional body.

Question: "The emotional body is the fourth body?"

The emotional body is linked with that of the Heart Chakra and the Throat Chakra. We move to what you have called the Third Eye. This is what is developing now, as you know, through Third to Fourth Dimension. Up to this point, mankind is highly developed up to this layer known as the throat area. He is merging now to understand the area within the Third Eye. It goes beyond the mental capability and the Mother Principle. This has represented the mind, that which collectively works with the other Chakras to form constructive use. But I say to you, this is the center and the body which must be developed to allow telepathic communication from other Star Systems. And this is the body that works as a sensing organism for harmony and cooperation among the masses. This is also the body which is sensitive to the collective force, that which is called the mass consciousness. Do you understand?

Question: "Yes, when you speak of us developing this area, will it just happen or is there a method that can be used?"

This is an area that you may develop on a personal basis but its development also relies heavily on the collective mass consciousness around you. This occurs on a 240 kilometer radius. That is why there is the deep need for one person to live in one area, for the development of this body and center.

Question: "Are there areas that are more conducive to developing the Third Eye?"

Of course, it is easier to develop this in quiet and secluded areas. It would explain why in the past, enlightened Avatars have traveled to mountaintops and to areas of seclusion. It, of course, depends on the basis set from your genetic coding and the acceleration into Cellular Awakening. Use of Violet Flame is encouraged for the development of this and as stated in past discourses, this is of vast importance. And so, we move to the point emerging, that which is a body known as the Gate. It is a gate which opens and closes. It is the pivot point between the Mother and Father Principle. It is a body which, once mastered and understood, allows you to travel between these two worlds. Do you understand?

Question: "Yes, will that also be developed?"

There are some upon the planet at this time who have developed all of these bodies, those which are members of the root race known as the Fifth Manu. You are members of this race and are being prepared for not only what you have known as the Third Eye Center but also that of the last remaining center [chakra] which corresponds in your physical plane. Do you have questions?

Question: "Can you develop these Chakras to travel through the gateway, as you put it, between the different awarenesses?"

This is our work on the planet at this time. It is for the alignment of these energies. As we enter into the period of alignment, known as the period of harmony and cooperation, our information on travel will come forth as a cosmic ray. You must understand, it is not a matter of development; this is a matter of natural cause. There is nothing that will stop this. It is just so. There are times that this development is delayed but a delay is an interval in time.

Question: "How does this effect the Earth as the Earth is also going through the same development as mankind? Where is the Earth in the development of those different layers that correspond to the Chakras?"

The Earth follows this in the pattern of the mass consciousness. All readings are taken from what is known as the sixth body, the collective body. As man's body has been formed of the earth substance, the actions through Spirit form a collective consciousness of the Earth.

Question: "So, all people on Earth will eventually evolve to that point?"

This is so and there are many upon the planets who are doing that at this instant. They are those who are able to read the Earth, to feel the Earth. They are those who have said "1 feel this in my bones." It is an old adage, I know, but yet, it is what is known as the Cellular Awakening, that of understanding your cells becoming ONE with the Mother Principle and verbalizing this, the Father Principle, and taking a course of action.

Question: "What do you mean by 'taking course of action'?"

We are speaking of right use of will, for through the merging of the Mother and the Father Principle, there has been given the gift of freewill. This has occurred along with the development of the emotional body. To that point, freewill is not allowed to enter into the consciousness. At the development of the emotional body, freewill is allowed to come forth.

Question: "So as we develop, the Earth follows right along with us? The density will be less?"

There is also the freewill of the planet. One must understand this. She too has her freewill and may step forward to say, "I will not offer myself any longer." She has been patient. As you move from this level of Third to Fourth Dimension, we would like to discuss the principles of Prahna, the Prahnic level, that which is the universal substance we draw upon. This is associated with the Cellular Awakening. The Earth itself is also coming to the awareness of such and draws out to the collective force, that which is other Solar Systems, planets, that which you have perceived as life from other systems. You call out to the collective force, other beings like yourself.

This sonar wave is registered as a sound frequency, a vibration associated with .28. You call to yourself, that which is associated with your seed group. You have noticed, upon the Earth Plane at this time, those who have collectively called out to receive this family, to become with that and merge with that. There is much discourse and discussion about that which you term the alien forces. And what they truly are, are your seed groups, your Brothers. There are even those that you have discussed as the Grey Men, those of the dualistic nature. They, too, are your Brothers. However, they have yet to function with what you know as the Heart Center, the emotional body.

They too have planted seeds upon your planet and those are the ones they come to claim. They have planted their seeds and they have, through the course of embodiment upon the planet, developed this center, the emotional body. And those that are drawn to information of that nature are receiving, through the finer energies, the development of the sixth body, the Cellular Awakening, calling them to become one with their Brothers. And so you understand, there is really no fight, as you perceive, or a struggle for higher and lower, there is only different vibration. But when one recognizes how this works together as one unit, one no longer perceives a struggle or perceives resistance but recognizes one as such, separate to one as such. You are comparing, in a sense, one color to another color. However, as we merge through this sixth body, you begin to understand that all is color. Do you understand, Dear ones?

Response: "Yes. In the past, there were problems with that, in that some people used other people because of lack of use of the Heart Chakra."

This is true. And there are star groups which have been seeded upon the planet that came with the emotional body functioning already. There are those who came without it.

Question: "We're all of us planted, so to speak, from other Galaxies, other planets?"

There is but one race that exists upon the Earth, which has risen up from the Earth itself. It is that known as the Aborigine. They are the true Earth race. Aside from that, Dear ones, you are all seeded. You have come to this planet to learn and to grow, to prepare you for other realms of consciousness, aside from the fact that you also embody in parallel dimensions and, beyond that, parallel universes. However, we will not overwhelm you with that information at this time. We hope you will grasp a firm understanding of these principles and understand, Dear ones, "as above, so below."

Question: "I would like to ask, as our bodies change, will there be a lot of pain? It seems to me that the Earth is in a lot of pain right now or she seems to be reacting quite violently in a lot of areas. Will our bodies change drastically as well?"

It is important that you understand, it is just a reaction to this natural cause of Cellular Awakening. It is perceived as pain through the genetic code, that which is associated with third level, the third level body. However, as one becomes more in alignment with the electromagnetic current that runs through the cosmos, one will notice a slackening off of what is perceived as pain. You will run much more smoothly, as that of a well-oiled gear, for as the gear begins to turn, it is rusty. And as you begin to move with all of these gears lined up, on to the next, you will experience a much smoother working of the mechanism.

Question: "Is this happening already?"

This is indeed happening and has always been occurring. These principles that I have explained are nothing new. They have occurred through age and age and age.

Question: "I was talking about the awakening processes, have they already begun?"

Yes, they have occurred. There have been those who were seeded upon the planet, who walked much more quickly through this. They came with a much higher alignment, or let me rephrase that, they came with alignment. There are those of you who too have come seeded with alignment and have decided to interbreed with those of other Star Seeds and altered your alignment. As you understand, the genetic coding is associated with that of the Cellular Awakening. Do you understand?

Question: "Yes. Is there anyone of pure family? Or is everyone more or less interbred?"

There are those that are of a pure family, as you would understand, in terms of pure alignment. This is not a race issue. This is an issue related to seed group.

Question: "So within each seed group, there might be black, yellow, red, and white people?"

Through the course of history, as man has perceived history, it has been the intermingling that has created the race. Dear ones, we wish not to discuss the race issue at this time and will save it for future discourse.

Question: "Could I ask about the weather patterns that are going on locally?"

Yes. And my Brother, Beloved Sananda, will step forward.

Welcome, my Sisters, I AM Sananda. I bring you a message of joy and peace, and I AM here for your loving assistance.

Question: "Welcome. We would like to ask about the weather, the local patterns, and maybe elsewhere. Have the Earth Changes begun?"

My Dear, we are in a period time known as Transition. I have prepared this feast, I invite you to sup with me. This is a time of great joy and your hearts are to be lightened. It is a time that you are being prepared to move Home. You are indeed the Prodigal Son and welcomed this time with a gladdened heart.

Question: "When you speak of moving Home, I feel that you are saying that there is no fear of the Earth Changes but simply, we're getting our bodies changed to be able to return to, maybe, another planet? Or is this moving into another awareness?"

It is moving into another awareness, into your collective groups, returning home to the Father's House, as it has been spoken of in past times. You are moving to what is known as the Father's House.

Question: "Is this simply spiritual or is this physical as well?"

It is both, my Dear ones. It is both. As you enter into the Transition, they assist one another and work with one another. You see, Dear ones, it is not a matter of giving up of the physical, it is a matter of mastering the physical to understand the Mother Principle, to honor and nourish this Mother Principle. For if you were Father Spirit, seeded into this universe without the Mother Principle, you would go without direction. You would indeed be light but you would not be the directed light. This is the work that you do. Do you understand the responsibility for the light you carry, to direct it through constructive use, the right use of your will? And also, do you understand the will of the creative force within you, to align yourself to that of Divine Purpose?

And so at this point, which is a quickening, we enter into what is known as Divine Service, extending to others what is within you. This is the work of integration of the Mother and Father Spirit, the Spirit within you. This is a quickening, a time to rejoice, for you have been called Home.

Question: "You talked about seed families. Does this mean that we will be gathering in like families, I mean in our own family units?"

Not only upon the Earth, throughout the cosmos, through the collective Logoic Web. These are indeed gateways or portals, as you have perceived them, through which we interconnect with that of the soul Source.

Question: "Are there also gateways on the Earth, physical as well as mental and spiritual?"

Indeed there are and they too interconnect with a cosmic nervous system, as you would perceive.

Question: "Are they Vortices?"

Yes, these are Vortices, understood to be the nervous system of the body and closely related to what is know as the heart body, the heart function on man. Do you understand? It is related to the emotional system.

Now he is showing the Earth in front of me. There are beams of light all over. He's showing what resembles the Aura of the Earth.

I bring you joy. I AM Sananda.

12

Sound vibration is present in all forms
of physical manifestation, including the physical body.
Certain sounds assist us to express our authentic, spiritual light.

Sound Technology and Sound Teachings

Saint Germain
Soltec
Sananda
Mary
Anaya

More people in our region are aware that I am channeling on a weekly basis, and when they call our office, Sherry often invites them to join us at her kitchen table. The following lesson is the result of one such invitation. A small group of spiritual seekers from Sandpoint drove down for the day to sit and ask questions. Interestingly, a new Spiritual Teacher joins us—a Pleiadian Goddess of scientific and spiritual knowledge who sends her telepathic message from over 440 light years away. Anaya's golden presence may be the result of the new "sitters," as her spiritual energy may more easily fit their energies and perhaps they are spiritually ready to hear her specific message. Or, it may be that her frequencies readily fit my more developed abilities to channel and capacity to relay information. In either case, both scenarios are likely true, and I am discovering that the more trance-work I do, well, the easier it gets.

The following lesson introduces the science of sound and how specific vowels relate to different Chakras. This is especially interesting, as the foundational teachings on the HUE vibration are communicated and this is one of the sacred names of God that invokes the energies of the Violet Flame. Anaya introduces advanced teachings on the Higher Self and how we can further integrate its spiritual knowledge for telepathic communication.

❧

Welcome, Beloved chelas, I AM Saint Germain. I am here this morning for your assistance and welcome you as Brothers and Sisters to the table. For this Time of Planetary Transition, it is of vast importance to become aware of the internal messages that are sent to you through your Higher Self, and bring you to a point of collective reasoning. We are speaking of the collective mind, that which is the collective force. This is brought forth, as you know, as many joining to ONE, to find a collective answer to the many issues surrounding your work upon the planet. As you are individualized in your path, you find these answers so you may move forth with great force, sometimes spiraling into the universe to find these answers. This is what we have referred to in past channelings or discourses as the Cellular Awakening. For you see, the Cellular Awakening occurs not only on an individual basis, but also on a collective basis. That is a reason to move into community or group, for as you move within these groups, you obtain a quickening, that which is known as the collective Cellular Awakening.

It is important at this time for you to understand this principle, of taking this and moving into the collective groups, as well as your individualized path. For it has been said that you walk hand in hand with your Brother and yet you choose of your freewill to take his hand and to walk with him. "Where two or more are gathered in the name," this is a universal principle, as above so below. This, I am sure you understand and give great reverence to it.

I would like to introduce to you, those available for discourse. I introduce my Dear Sister, Beloved Kuan Yin, my Brother Soltec, and that which is known as a world leader at this Time of Planetary Transition, my Beloved Brother Sananda. We are most happy to assist you and open the floor for your questions. Again, I ask that we have your permission to give our assistance, for we have spoken about the use of freewill and ask for your permission.

Response: "Yes."

We are most delighted to serve you and eagerly await your questions.

Question: "I'd like to ask about sound technology and its use in the healing process?"

My Dear one, I would like to introduce you to my Brother Soltec, for much of his information has dealt with this technology.

Greetings, Brother of the Flames, I AM Soltec. I come forth to assist you in this technology. Your question?

Question: "We have become involved with the sound, magnetic, and color therapies and I'd like to know a little bit more about them in the healing process."

As you have become aware of the seven points available upon the human body, you must also become aware of the seven points available upon the Earth Planet itself. The corresponding nature of each of the seven points to the seven points upon the planet itself are with the Rays of Divine Guidance, Divine Truth, Divine Wisdom, Divine Love, Divine Abundance and Prosperity, also that of Divine Transformation. As you have seen, as these centers open, they integrate, one into the other. However, as we deal with the properties of electromagnetism and the properties related to color, also understood as high frequency sound, these correspond to one another and serve one another. It is the true healing process, to integrate these into one.

There is technology to align these at this time, measuring the chakric energy as you have understood, with that of the chakric energy of the Earth. For you see, within the rocks, the water and the winds, there are properties too, of electromagnetism and of color and sound vibration. Each center corresponds with a specific sound. You have within your English language, the A,E,I,O,U, each of these, bringing forth a sound resonance corresponding with a color vibration. "A" corresponds with the lower Chakra, most associated with red and brown. "E' is associated with the next Chakra Center and that of the yellow vibration. "I" is associated with the third and the color associated with this is green. We move to what is called the fourth center, the "U," the heart, which is closely associated with two color-sound vibrations, green and pink. Again, as you have known, the Throat Chakra Center corresponds to the blue intensity, also surrounded with golden light as well. It is the blending of these two with the sound harmonic. Moving on to the next Chakra Center, we give you the color purple mixed with that of yellow, and on to the Crown, which is the merging of all colors into what is known as white Christic light. It is the Crown Center which also combines all these sounds into one sound, one common sound.

I would suggest for you to run these sound vibrations, play them simultaneously, for you to understand the Vibration of the Crown Chakra. There are those centers which correspond with this on the Earth as well. Have I explained myself?

Question: "Yes. I'd like one clarification. The vowel sound of "U," you're saying relates to the fourth Chakra, the Heart Chakra, the green and pink?"

More specifically, we refer to the HUE sound vibration, which has a relationship directly to what you have known in past cultures as the OM. There has been information upon the planet that the HUE vibration is for leaving the realm of consciousness, to travel into what mankind has known as the astral. We would like to give you further information on the HUE vibration. The HUE is associated with the Heart Center and forms a point .486 kilometers in front of this heart center, forming a circle radius around the body. It serves for, what we have referred to, as the Cellular Awakening. [Clerical Note: There was some hesitation over the use of the word "kilometer." I feel that the word "meter" may have been the measurement that Soltec was scanning Lori's language banks for. .486 is equal to approximately 1594 feet in kilometers, whereas .486 is equal to approx. 18 1/2 inches in meters. The following are equivalent measurements: 1.0 kilometers = .621 miles, 5280 feet = 1.0 mile, 1.0 meter = 39.37 inches.]

Question: "You talked about the gyroscopic device, which is a high frequency. What about the low frequency?"

This is where we introduce the principle of the Mother, that of which the body is comprised upon Earth, as you know her. As she has brought forth herself, to offer her assistance for your planetary embodiment, these are the lower frequencies. These serve as a point of generation of electromagnetic current, to allow light to enter into the system and sound vibration to resonate within. And so, upon your planet, there has been the use of stone and water. However, there are higher properties associated with these, to bring forth total integration of the Chakra Centers.

Question: "I am particularly interested in the Rife technology, which uses low frequency sound for the breakdown of various crystalline structures."

You must be aware, my Dear one, that sound vibration is carried through all things and there is an actual registration of sound even within a simple rock or a simple plant. This is measurable and would assist and accompany this work you speak of.

Question: "Are you saying to use the Rife, you should also incorporate the other sound and color, in order to be complete?"

The lower density sound vibrations work with the cleansing of elements within the life stream of the body. The higher frequencies deal with your spiritual self, the spiritual body. Each contains complementary properties, one to another. For you see, in universal laws and principles, we stress as "above, so below," and the same in the construction of the human body, the physiology, as it accompanies that of the spiritual essence. We work for the integration of these two centers.

He's going to a blackboard now, drawing two circles and showing how they merge together and putting another mathematical equation near the two circles, 5.87/7C3.17.

Question: "What does that particular formula mean and what is it in relationship to?"

This particular formula is the relationship of integration of Elemental chakric forces to the spiritual electromagnetic forces, the point of merger for collective reasoning. You have well known that what you think upon, you become. We have simply broken this into a mathematical equation for your use and research.

Question: "What I'd like to move on to now is the work of Tesla. I am interested in becoming more involved with the technology of free energy. Where can I get more information about that in the work that is being passed on and actually being done through the Tesla group of people that are on the planet?"

He is talking to some other people and indicating that there are several centers in the central coastline area of California. There is also one in Denver, one on the East Coast, one someplace in Maryland, and one in Canada.

Question: "Do we need these machines for the healing process or can we do the work ourselves, through prayer?"

As in all things, the intent of the soul, desiring to serve, operates through the highest vibration and motivation. It is our desire to impart technology to accelerate this desire of service. Of course, this can be done through prayer. It is a simpler path. We impart technologies to assist those who have not only the need for energy release, as you have known it, but releasing energy blockages. Blockages have occurred not only through previous embodiment, but also as one emerges from genetic memory to Cellular Awakening. Do you understand?

Question: "Yes. Is there more on Tesla, about free energy, but also about energy gravitational devices and transportation?"

He is showing me the planet and it is surrounded by a belt of energy.

This belt of energy which surrounds your planet contains within it an energy source known as freonic elements, comprising a twelve-sided triangle. It is a generative force which works collectively.

Question: "Is there anyone working with this technology at the moment?"

He's laughing and indicating that it is you!

My Dear Brother, I AM here for your assistance and ask for you to call to me through your freewill. I will prepare a path for individuals to be placed before you, to continue this research and work that is of high interest to you. There are indeed many working upon this technology, as it is dispensed to mankind and we will lovingly prepare a path for this to occur.

He is projecting his hands toward you. He's standing at your back and placing his hands on your shoulders. He's preparing to leave.

Response: "Thank you, Soltec."

It is my pleasure to serve you and turn the floor to Beloved Saint Germain.

My Beloveds, this day I introduce to you, my Sister Kuan Yin.

Dear hearts, I bring my message to you, to the planet. And as you move to your groups of collective reasoning, I ask but one thing, to love one another, to simply love one another, to look upon the face of humanness and see within them, that which is the desire to serve. Love one another.

They just left. I'll rest a minute and go back in. Mary steps forward.

Brothers and Sisters, I welcome you with grace. And it is with great joy, I come to you. I AM Mary and I have come this day for your assistance and to speak to you of the Principles of Grace. As you work upon the planet, it is also of vast importance, that you work with joy, joy in your heart for the work you do. Take this work and nurture it as you would a babe, holding it in your arms, swaddling it in the cloth of light, nurturing it with the warm cloak of your soul. Become a part of it and let it become a part of you, an extension of yourself, as you walk this path of grace.

There are times you feel pushed and there are times you feel driven. How can you push and drive such a thing? How can you push or drive this child brought to you, for you to raise and become a part of your family. You take it lovingly into your arms and hold it and accept it. There are times through this work, you do feel yourself stumbling and falling, with tears upon your cheek. It is time to brush these tears aside and see this great birth that comes forth. See the joy of this Immaculate Conception that comes through Co-creation with this God Force, that you are indeed a part of it and have extended yourself to this. My Dear ones, I bless you in your work and bless you in your path.

She's stepping back and another lady is stepping forward.

I welcome you. My name is Anaya. I come to assist you in understanding, not only that of science and technology, but that of the higher principles that underlie all that is said and done. We speak of the motivational forces, that which is the sincere desire to serve. There are times, as one enters into planetary service that they feel a great need and void within themselves and so perform this service. And in doing so, this void or separation becomes smaller and smaller and the gateways and portals begin to open. Others are placed in your path, for you to merge and become ONE with. There are also those that you must say, "not at this present moment." I AM here to answer your questions.

Question: "I'd like to ask how the body corresponds with the Earth. We were all having pains and stomach aches and feeling ill last night. Was this because the Earth was going through some particular event such as earthquakes or volcanoes or something?"

My Dear, not only is the Earth in upheaval in transitory events, what you have experienced is the nova effect of a planetary system and the Earth was impacted by the energy of this collective force. You see, there are other such systems that exist and their energy and thought waves affect your planet, as well as the effect of your planet upon them.

Question: "Will our body be able to tell us what events are going on at any particular time? Does it correspond?"

You sense and see and hear and smell. These have been given to you as receptors of energy in the human physiology and of course, in dealing with that of the genetic coding. There are those which are keener and more developed. Our concern is for you to use this physical body you have been given, to express that which is the eternal light body, that which is the spiritual essence. For you see, without the spiritual essence, you are unable to use the receptor, which is known as the physical body.

At night, as you use your true body, you bring forth information that is received through the receptors during the day. You sense, not only your planet but other Galaxies, Solar Systems, and Planetary Systems. Many of you travel to these other places at night and some of you travel during the day. Unaware of that portion of yourself, known as the true spiritual body, the Higher Self, the I AM Presence, it remains intact as a spiritual force and travels to sense and to bring back to you in the physical. You may be awake at this time and sense yourself being full and comfortable within your body, however, this is a portion of you that remains.

When you experienced physical discomfort, what occurred was an explosion of that planetary system, which was long overdue and expected. You have simply sensed it and brought it forth. It does indeed affect the Earth Plane and the Planet. If you were to feel this in the body, through what you have known as the centered energy of the body, it is that which has been taken, out of trust from the womb. Do you understand?

Question: "As we were out-of-body, sensing what's going on, then it affects our physical body?"

There are those indeed more sensitive, who through agreement have allowed this portion of themselves to retain and travel, even through the waking hours, to send this message. We are speaking of a split that has occurred of the energies of the Higher Self, forming a communicative network. This is what has been known as the intuition. Of course, you have experienced many who have a great intuition. They have simply entered into a split of the collective consciousness of the Higher Self and allowed its retention to come forth through the apex center, the Higher Source hovering approximately twelve to twenty feet above the physical body. And so, as an umbrella effect, this split consciousness travels and retains and brings forth. We are also speaking about the parallel dimensions of time, the ability to split within these dimensions and travel to these. This again comes through the Higher Source. Do you understand?

Response: "Yes."

There are those who have agreed to not allow this to occur, those who have taken a more direct stance to integrate fully with the Higher Source. And there are those who have agreed to split the Higher Source. Mankind has perceived this as phenomena, however, this is not so. All are blessed with the gift of intuition. However, some have simply chosen to allow the Higher Self to be fully utilized to a capacity. There are those who have chosen a more directed force and would not speak of intuition but only of what they are. Do you understand?

Question: "Are those who have split and allowed a part of themselves to be used, aware of the pains in the body? Are those, that are totally involved, the ones who are experiencing this?"

There are energy points upon the system as the Higher Self splits and travels to dimensions, as well as parallel universes. There are the points upon the body that correspond to this. Have you not met a person who is highly sensitized to the body system? It appears this person is always at disease. This person, who has merely allowed, through the sleep state, the splitting of the consciousness, experiences the energy the following day. Do you understand?

Question: "Now, we have a question about communicating with animals. How best can we do this, in order to know their needs and for them to know ours?"

Most of the animals upon your planet work with sound vibration. You carry within your Auric Field, a sound vibration that harmonizes or blends with that of the sound vibration of that particular species. There are those who adjust their frequencies quite readily and easily through sound and there are those who resonate with one particular sound. There are those who communicate through this sound resonance and there are those who do not. It is important to understand your sound and to feel, harmonize, and blend this with more species, for you to investigate other sounds and for you to become comfortable with such. The pitch of your voice is also the pitch of your Auric Field. Do you understand?

Question: "What about mental communication?"

Of course, all communication occurs at the field of the Higher Self. It is only that which we are drawing into the mind of the body. This is the misconception of man, that communication comes through the brain, this is not so. It only serves as a tool, to relay it. True communication comes through the Higher Self, to be split or opened through the Higher Self, so you may share this. There is also that of communication of one individual to the other. That again involves the splitting of the energies of the Higher Self to that of the individual you would wish to perform this function with. Do you understand?

Question: "Yes. Are there any messages you'd like to leave with us?"

My message, as a member of the planet Pleiades, is that you remember that your body is not real, that your physical forces around you have been great gifts to exemplify your spirit. You are spiritual beings and it is of vast importance that you understand this, that your body and your Earth have been given to you to express spirit. You are spiritual beings, honor thy Spirit within yourself. See these bodies around you, not as bodies, but as those which are spirit. You live and walk and breathe in the world of Spirit and this one message I bring to you.

Question: "Thank you. Did Sananda have anything to say? He was around earlier."

They're together. The only thing he said was "Bless You."

13

It is a joy to sense and feel.
All is Spirit—all is source.

From the Golden Beam

Anaya

The oppressive heat of the day often lifts during the summer night and I sit on the front porch in the early evening listening to crickets sing and air conditioners hum while the kids play, turning cartwheels in the grass and chasing one another. The sky is alight with brilliant, glowing stars and I wonder where in this glittering galaxy are the seven planets of the Pleiades—also known as the Seven Sisters? In this session, the beautiful golden goddess from the celestial sisters appears and reveals her insights on possible Earth Change and humanity's spiritual movement into the ONE. As I enter into trance, I see a golden light creating a geometric matrix comprising eight converging lines. Anaya's sublime consciousness moves through this pattern of light and joins our conversation.

I AM here, my Beloved Sister, for your assistance. I have been brought forth through the portal of light, known as the Golden Beam. I come to impart my message to you. I AM Anaya and I have come to bring greater clarity to the messages you receive through that which is known as the Hierarchal Eight, that which is brought forth on the Vibration of the Golden Ray, beaming forth to life streams during this Time of Transition. We serve upon this Council to impart this knowledge to you, to assist you in attaining a one-to-one relationship with the Higher Self, to bring it closer to your own presence, so you will no longer need to ask for our assistance but go to that of the Higher Self. We ask for the collective merging, not only of the Higher Self, but for you to merge with our vibration and to feel us and to become ONE with us.

There is much happening upon your planet, as you are well aware, not only the shift of the Earth Plane but the shift of the Planet. You are being readied, you see, to move into a new reality of dimensional consciousness and it is our hope that we may prepare you for such. We may do as much work as possible in relaying these words to you, relaying these thoughts and sending our vibrations to you, however, it is of vast importance that you reconnect with that which is your Source. For this is our mission, to reconnect you to your Source, so you may function as a full God Being. You see, this is what you have termed as the separation. However, we see it more as aligning the mathematical structures, not only within the physical body, but within the spiritual body, for you to come forth as God Beings. Beloveds, I AM here for your assistance.

Question: "Are you alone today?"

I have come forth on what is known as the Pattern of Eight. A path has been prepared for me to come through to serve and assist you, for you see, Dear ones, there are times that I too cloak myself within the physical body and come forth in embodiment. My vibration would be known to be denser as sorts. It was felt, at this time, because of my close association with density and matter, that which you call the human vibration, that I could assist you much in understanding the raising of the body, the finer energies within the body and the electromagnetic currents which run within the cells. For you to understand proper alignment through many modes, we ask you to not squeeze this force from these cells but for it to be awakened, to be taken and realigned and readjusted for you to use. For you see, the challenge is Mastery of these cells. Of course, there are times when I AM aligning mine as well. I have come as, one would call, a bridge.

Question: "Please give us an overview on the present Earth situation."

It is imperative that the message of Earth is brought forth to mankind, for indeed she will suffer her cataclysmic Earth Changes if one does not realize the spiritual path of life, the spiritual way of being. All is Spirit and that as you move through matter, you must honor and respect this in all that you do, all that you see, all that you are. This is the challenge brought to mankind. For you see, mankind forgets the Source.

You see Dear ones, life is indeed sacred and what a joy to be upon the planet. What a beautiful place to come, to see, to smell, and to feel. What a gift it is to have these bodies and yet there are many within this movement who would like to eliminate these bodies. This body has been given to you as a great gift. It is a joy to be able to be ONE with spirit. If man would but understand that it is a joy to have embodiment. It is a joy to be ONE with the Elemental natures. It is a joy to take a walk within a forest and to touch and to smell and to breathe the air. This is the message, to rejoice in what you have been given. This is a matter of rapture of the moment, to totally encase all that you are and to recognize the other portions that you are. There is, indeed, a deeper intrinsic meaning in all that you are. It is important that this message go forth, that all is Spirit. And as man moves through this collective way of being, he begins to understand that all is Spirit and then he is able to reconnect to that which is the Source and express this Source in all his activities.

Question: "In order to live in the physical world and think that all is spiritual, you still have to pay money for food and a place to live; will that be taken care of?"

Perhaps the most dangerous part of man at this time is that which is called the mind. For you see, the mind functions, not in Spirit and not in physical. It is the mind that encases and tortures man, his thoughts. Do you understand?

Question: "Yes. In other words, fear comes into the mind and the mind then takes over?"

It penetrates the flesh and allows the penetration of Spirit. For you see, it is the mind that you have come to release and to give to the Spirit. We are not saying that there is not Divine Wisdom, wisdom which is known as Divine Order. It is indeed the mind that man must learn to release, for the thoughts, the constant steady thoughts, the tinkering within this realm of being, is one which has the tendency to encase fear and bring it forth within reality.

Question: "So, we're to trust our feelings and our senses and just goes with whatever, not think it over."

To be, this is the point. To be who you are. I AM always, in love, Anaya.

14

*Earth is a beautiful and nurturing home, where we learn
to identify illusion and the gift of our freewill.*

Feminine Principle

Saint Germain
Portia
Kuan Yin
Mary

On a beautiful June morning Sherry drops by my house. The kids had been attending summer Bible school at a local church, and I welcomed the free time for myself. "Do you have an hour?" I detect that look in her eye . . . I know we're off for an adventure. Before I can even nod, I've grabbed my purse and find myself climbing into the passenger seat of her station wagon.

"I've got something to show you. I think you'll find it most interesting," says Sherry, and we drive for about thirty minutes through the little town of Asotin and upriver along the Snake River. We drive past small farms and orchards, and, before long, Sherry pulls the car over and parks off of the gravel road. The river swirls before me like an unseen Vortex, and I sense a strong electromagnetic energy. Sharp basalt rocks polished by the winds and rains of time jut out on both sides of the pulsing river adding to the intense energy. I follow Sherry as she hikes down a graveled path. No doubt, she knows where she's going.

"See," she points, and the outline of petroglyphs emerges in the sunlight, and as my eyes adjust to their subtle etching, I see that the rocks are peppered with dozens of them. They certainly convey a story from another time, and my senses are alive with excitement. This is a sacred site.

"See this one." She points to a figure—likely a shaman—and he holds a long stick or pole with two circles on either end. The figure literally takes my breath away. It looks exactly like the archtometer that Saint Germain showed me in visions and trance-work well over a year ago! "Looks just like it, doesn't it?" says Sherry. She lights a cigarette and an intense expression comes over her face as she blows the smoke into the bright, clear air. "I think we should ask them what this is about."

I nod and follow her to a basalt ledge where we sit down and absorb the magnificent energies of the swirling forces and the river's mysterious eddy. I feel transported out of time and space.

Later that evening Lynne shows up for the weekly channeling, and before long there is another knock on the door and Glenda walks in. This lesson gives new definition to the petroglyphs, and according to Saint Germain, this was an entrance area for ancient space travelers and their technologies were literally able to open the skies while simultaneously aligning the Earth's energy fields without any negative ramification.

Apparently sacred sites such as this are peppered everywhere on Earth and help us to remember our true self—the divine Source.

We call together to our mighty I AM Presence, our Higher Self, to the Spiritual Hierarchy of the Great White Brotherhood. We call for you to enlighten us and to send your messages to help us learn and assist us on this path that is life. We ask that everything you bring to us is brought through the Christ Spirit and the White Light and brings us a deeper understanding of our spiritual self. Thank you.

Greetings, Children of the Flame, I AM Saint Germain. I AM here for your assistance and will facilitate this meeting. Present is my Beloved Sister Kuan Yin, my Beloved Sister Mary, my Divine Compliment, Portia. We are here today to discuss what is called the Feminine Principle, that which is understood in the planet and represented from the planet as the material form of being. What is this concept that we speak of? The Feminine Principle has been associated with feeling, that which is known to you as intuition, that which is also understood in the body in the lower Chakra energy points. It is the point of conception. It is also the womb of nurturing.

You look at this planet that you live on, this Earth Plane and Planet, and question your presence. You have been brought to this planet to understand not only many aspects of yourself and interaction of the aspects of others, but also to understand the principles of the feminine planet. It is individualized in this femininity, brought forth as a nurturing place. We have referred to it as the Garden. Throughout the ages, there have been many periods of time that the Garden is harvested. This is the Time of Transition, the time when the Garden is ready to be harvested. You enter into the Garden and you see it the way it is. You take the fruit that is ready to be harvested. You go into the Garden and select what is appropriate for you to take. You see the weeds and you see the thorns and you walk around them. Do you understand?

Question: "Yes. You are referring to the harvest that's going to take place on the Earth, of the people?"

This is precise. And you yourself must harvest that which is appropriate for you. You are brought to this Point of Transition now to choose. You walk in the garden and decide what is appropriate for your individualized path. We speak much of the path of perfection and indeed perfection is attainable at many levels. Perhaps, to explain this in a much more simple way, we are speaking of the perfection of the physical body and your world of material illusion. You are here to perfect illusion. We understand that this is a concept hard for you to perceive but many of the illusions are brought to you so that you can understand how the material world is illusive. Through the understanding of illusion, you are brought to the point of your Mastery of the material. Do you understand?

Question: "Yes. As an illusion, will smoking hurt the body or can we Master that as well. Is the body harmed for the transition by cigarettes?"

Of course, it clouds your thoughts and thinking but it is the mind that perceives this.

Question: "So we believe, so it is?"

As you move in the field of material illusion, you must recognize all things as temporary and all things as instantaneous. Perhaps you perceive a rock to be solid and yet, the rock can easily be shattered and be made into many small pebbles. This is the truth. And so, you are here to choose how you wish to be. It is an illusion, I know, my Dear Children, for there are many choices for you to make, many paths for you to follow. I AM here for your assistance.

Question: "If the Earth is an illusion and our bodies are illusion, it seems they become manifest by thought form. Do thought forms of the masses create the problems on Earth?"

You are speaking of what is called the collective thought.

Question: "How much collective thought goes into our bodies and ourselves? Is that just principally our thoughts?"

It would be impossible for you to embody upon the physical plane without an effect of collective thought form. For you see, Dear one, this is what you have come to experience. You experience collective thought form, which has been understood as a point of time, as you call history, that which you call an era or epoch. You choose this period of time, a point of reference for you to experience the collective form.

Question: "So in other words, in each era or time or place, there are certain rules that go along with the illusion?"

Perhaps I can best explain this way. It is your thought that is most powerful. If your thoughts linger upon joy, you will become joyous. Mankind has perceived this as negative and positive. We simply perceive it as a term we call the dynamic parallel. You see, you are here to experience many things, so that you may choose where you would prefer to be.

Question: "So what feels right and what we focus on, we become?"

This is exactly the truth. It is also important for you to understand that you are choosing.

Question: "The Earth has a freewill, which is also affected like our freewill?"

She too has made her choice to nurture mankind at this period in time. There is much talk about the heart and the concept of the heart, that which gives freely and unconditionally. But it too functions through choice. The mind has been given to you as a great tool, to choose to use the heart. A heart that does not use the mind, gives with free abandon and its energy is wasted and dissipated. But the heart that gives through choice and has proceeded through Divine Intelligence opens to the clear use of giving. We are speaking of directed individualized energy force.

Response: "I would like to thank you, Saint Germain, for helping me get started with my card project."

I have enjoyed the project myself. It has been long since I have had the opportunity to participate in such a project. I AM thankful for the opportunity to Co-create in material form. I too, at my state of being, make the choice. You see, the choice is the point for materialization and dematerialization. Do you understand?

Question: "Yes. We were talking of going to the mountain that is Swallow's Nest and of doing an Earth Healing. Would this be of help to the Earth or to the area?"

Of course this is. You have been called upon to adjust the energy there.

Question: "Is there a procedure for adjusting energy or will we be guided to do the correct procedure?"

As we have spoken of choice, this is indeed your choice to do so. We would be glad to assist in this. Perhaps it is better to wait until you have had an opportunity to speak to her.

Question: "May I ask for clarification? Speak to her? Who, the Mother Earth?"

He's not saying.

Question: "I would like to ask then about Buffalo Eddy, the rock up the river, where there are petroglyph writings on the rock."

This is the remnants of, what you would refer to, a star base. It is a point of entry.

Question: "In the drawings, could you explain what the people are doing?"

They are aligning the energy field and system to this Earth Plane.

Question: "Aligning the Earth itself, or just the entry point?"

The entry point.

Question: "And these were one of the Star Seed groups?"

It was one of twelve.

Question: "One of twelve Star Seed groups, could you explain? In the pictures, there was a man or an entity, holding a rod with two rotating orbs or balls on either end. Was this for the same purpose that you gave Lori the technology that she has?"

Of course it is. This has been brought forth for your use and, as been stated previously, usage has not been allowed until your time. We purposely held back the information. You must understand, the planet itself must be properly aligned for the use of this. Not only will it adjust your frequency wave, its use is to allow those who will be coming. Do you understand?

Question: "Yes. Will this work after the first polar shift or will it be after the second or the third polar shift that it will be active?"

As all events are arbitrary in the world of illusion, it may happen instantaneously or it may take years to happen. Do you understand?

Question: "If you were to take a reading of the area today, do we have some time left to work on other things or should we be moving to higher ground now?"

He's holding in his hand a ball of light. He's blowing on it.

Question: "Do you blow the light from your Source away from yourself?"

No. You are to be near your Source. Do you understand? We are permitted to tell you much and yet there is your freewill.

Question: "Will we be guided or know if we've chosen to live and stay during the Time of Transition."

You are in the transition now.

Question: "And if we choose to live through it and help others, work with it and others, will we be guided to know what to do and when to do it?"

I assure you.

Question: "Could you tell me, Swallow's Nest, are we being drawn there because the Earth needs a healing or is it perhaps, when the transitions come, this will be an entry point for those who are coming?"

You are remembering the Source. I would prefer, my Dear ones, for you to travel to this point to do our work at that point.

Response: "All right."

Beyond the alignment of energies from this device, it serves to align the energies of those entering at that time. It is held within the left hand and spun no more than what you would perceive as four feet within the circle diameter.

He's showing a series of rings. Seven rings, seven adjustments and the number 22.

15

*Do not allow others' agendas to
interfere with your spiritual development.
Walk in your path; allow others to walk their path.*

Alignment
Saint Germain
Ehone

I've met a nice young man at a lunch date with a group of friends. I immediately know that he is attracted to me. He is younger than me and has two small children from a former marriage. As hypocritical as this may sound, I'm uncertain that I want to date anyone who has children. And he is deeply involved with his church. Not that I don't have respect for him for practicing his faith, but I know that once he discovers I'm involved with trance-work, well—there could be conflict.

Even though I've missed my own children during the school year, I've adapted to having time by myself, and more importantly, the crucial time to organize the trance-work and publish the I AM America Newsletter. Plus I've been organizing the transcripts and prophecies to write my first book.

He calls and asks me out—I was right! Now the conundrum of thoughts: should I say yes? David's calls have lessened in the last month. He is busy with his career and, while he is very interested in the work of the Ascended Masters, I am aware that he does not recognize my level of devotion to the I AM America teachings. I also sense a difference in our beliefs. David accepts channeled works, yet does not believe in them. This, too, could cause problems if we deepen our commitment to one another.

Sherry senses my conflict as I enter her house for a session. My life is such a stark contrast to hers: she has been married to Steve for over twenty years and her children are raised. I look out the window at her garden, with neatly planted rows of sprouting corn, zucchini, carrots, greens, and flowers—all well established. "Will I ever get it together?" I ask that question not only to her, but to myself; it's a question of self-worth, doubt, and confidence.

"You need to kiss a few frogs before you meet your prince." She points to a chair and I sit down while she lights a cigarette. "Before I met Steve, I was single for a long time." She draws the smoke in deeply, and exhales while talking. I sense emotional pain in her voice. "Keep your focus on your children right now . . . men come and go."

Perhaps the best way to understand the Spiritual Teachers' lesson on alignment is to grasp the idea of personal balance. As we spiritually evolve, we undoubtedly change. Saint Germain advises, "Do not take the beloved Flame in your heart and throw it to others." That is, don't try to make others understand something that they are not ready to understand, and may never be willing to comprehend. And don't compromise yourself.

In this lesson, Sherry and Saint Germain discuss Earth Changes and the potential to inspire the spiritual development of humanity. And this leads to teachings regarding our indelible connection to sacred sites and how they assist the process of spiritual alignment by balancing light-fields and Chakra Centers. This alignment process is not only spiritual but physical, and specific minerals in sacred locations can help the physical body to acclimate to subtle and finer energy. Saint Germain is clear that the spiritual process of integrating new energies is known as the Father Principle, and the physical process of our body absorbing this energy is known as the Feminine Principle.

Before the session ends, a beautiful Angel of Protection—Ehone—appears. I often question if I need protection, so I welcome his presence. His message is simple and profound: become a spiritual warrior for your own spiritual development. He reminds us: "Let no one walk in your path . . . and allow others to walk (in) theirs."

Welcome, my Beloved chela, I AM Saint Germain. I sense your purity of heart and I AM here for your assistance. As you have understood the right of freewill, I ask for your permission to give you such. Do I have your permission?

Response: "Yes."

I AM most delighted to serve you this morning and I come with the message of the Hierarchy. Cast not your pearls before swine. Do you understand the message of this? Do not take the Beloved flame within your heart and throw it to those who do not understand. Rather, gather it up to yourself and bring it forth within yourself and extend it to your Brother in Divine Service. For what is Divine Service but the extension of yourself to another. And how is this achieved? Through the Vibration of Love. Again, we have talked much about love. Love is a choice. It is indeed far from feeling, far from the world of emotion, as you call it. It is the choice that we have spoken about. Each day, you consciously make the choice to love your Brother and each day, you must consciously make the choice to love yourself. Each day you consciously make the choice to extend this work.

I AM here for your assistance and remind you of the use of the Violet Flame, that which is the Flame of Mercy and Forgiveness. For you see, within this flame is the Law of Grace. For as you encounter one another, those who come to you with their words, words that seem to attack you, words that seem to instill fear in you, this law, this golden Law of Mercy and Forgiveness is brought to set you free. It is the Law of Grace. I AM here for assistance, Dear ones, and welcome your discourse and questions.

Question: "I would like to ask some more about Earth Changes. I would like to ask how we will know where safe places are. Is this done by feeling? I was riding by a location the other day and I sensed it was to be changed and I felt physically ill."

Perhaps you were sensing an area that was not proper for your alignment, for we have spoken much of the alignment of the body. There is also the alignment of what we speak of as the spirit, your Spirit filled within your body. Do you not see that as the Spirit, or I AM Presence, as we have called it, fills and penetrates the body, your body searches to become aligned to particular geophysical areas, areas that enhance your being? There has been much discourse about the heart and during these times of cataclysmic change and movement, that the heart is indeed the fine record, the fine way of being.

Mankind worries much about the physical body and we are more concerned about that of his spiritual self. We understand your limitation of being in this body. You have been given a mind to judge or discern with, you have been given this body to walk upon this planet with, you have been brought here as a Divine Creation and as an extension of the world of Spirit. We have spoken much of feeling and now we must speak to that of being, as it was said, "to be or not to be." It is most important that during this Time of Planetary Transition that you be and enjoy your life, the life of Spirit. Do you not see?

Question: "Yes, I understand that the Spirit is the most important but that we are, in fact, physical. We are limited and search for ways to live in the physical realm. I get a lot of questions from people, Mr. L.T.; he asks why he was guided to go to the Teton Mountains? Could you shed any light on that?"

Again, there is that which is called the alignment, for as you are ready to receive, you are given the alignment. And as you give to this alignment, you are ready to receive. There is a fine balance that occurs between physical matter and the spirit, for indeed, the physical body is the densification of spirit. However, as you have understood it to be temporary, I would say that our work has just begun with this individual you have mentioned. There are indeed those areas of the Earth that one travels for alignment, alignment not only with that of the Earth itself but that which reaches through the cosmos and through other planetary systems. Each one carries within their fine blueprint, that which you would call a mission. For you see, you are all Divine Inheritors and as these children, you have come here to be. You have come to learn and you, above all, have come here to be an extension in service.

Question: "When we go to these areas to find alignment and to help ourselves align spiritually and physically, is there a process that we should go through when we align?"

Of course, prayer and meditation are of vast importance. It is important to anchor yourself to this area. Allow the golden beam of light that comes from your Higher Self through the Crown Chakra, to run down the spine as you sit at this particular location. I would ask, too, that you become familiar with the Earth at this location, for even within its soil and being, it has been penetrated with the molecular structures from the alignment with other planets. For you see, there are no mistakes and each location, as you walk on every square foot, is a mathematical calculation. And so, as you have been directed to travel to such a spot, you may take earth substance from this location, that which is aligned with you.

Question: "I have a friend who is traveling now. Is there a spot that she should travel to that will help her align, adjust to the Earth and her spiritual self?"

Of course, as you understand the Spirit and its entrance to the body, there are many areas that you may travel to. For you see, as the Higher Self integrates with that of physical, you begin to understand the Cellular Awakening. And through this Cellular Awakening, you move through various lands to be in specific locations.

We align our systems with properties of minerals. We also align ourselves, not only with the properties from the planet itself, but we align ourselves with the Divine Blueprint that has been sent from the cosmos, that penetrates these land areas. They allow for the freer flowing of the Higher Self and remove blockages. Of course, you also learn to sense this planet as a planetary organism, for your bodies are made up of her, as the Mother Principle. As you travel to each of these points, you feel the Father Principle, taking that which is the Mother from this area, as it is impregnated with that of the Father Principle.

Question: "The spiritual is the Father Principle; the physical is the Mother Principle?"

They are, of course, integrated as ONE. The Father Principle is spiritual and physical. The Mother Principle is spiritual and physical. But for the sake of clarity, we shall distinguish the two, the Father as spirit, the Mother as physical. This plane where they merge is that alignment for the self. Do you understand?

Question: "Yes, so there are many spots on the Earth that we can align with. How do we know when we're living in a spot that is not conducive for our growth? Do we become physically ill?"

It is important to observe your physical nature. Perhaps the most important organ to observe would be that of the skin. It is important for you to observe its reaction to each area. It is by far the most highly sensing organ on the body.

Question: "I wonder if we could talk about seeing Auras on others and sensing their well-being or their attitudes. How can you best learn to do this?"

It is important that you feel your own presence around you at all times. Of course, in daily living and being in that of the physical, you encounter many who have differing Auric Fields. There are many who walk, perhaps with a larger percentage of what is known as the Green Ray within their Auric Field and there are those who walk with what is known as the Pink Ray. There are those who do walk with such a small percentage of light within their field, it is abrasive to those who carry this light within their field. I would instruct you on the technique of the Tube of Light. Call to your Higher Self to bring this Tube of Light into your field and surround it with the Blue Flame. For you see, my Dear one, the Blue Flame comes from that of the Angelic Host, that which ministers directly with Elemental Life Force.

And now Beloved Ehone would like to take the floor.

Welcome my Children. My name is Ehone. I come to you with a message of strength. I ask for you to be strong in the work that you do. I ask for you to take your Sword of Light and carry it around you as a shield to protect yourself and to protect the work you do. There are many forces at work on the planet at this time. You perceive these as good and bad. You perceive dark and evil and light and good. But perhaps the message I say to you is to be strong within yourself and to carry the strength of your being in all that you do. I come forth to share the majesty of the Christ Spirit. I come forth from I AM THAT I AM. Do you not know that you are Children of God and are created from Him? You have come forth on this planet to express as Divine Inheritors. Each of you has the right to choose your expression and let no one take your inheritance from you.

Ehone is very tall, about eight feet. He vibrates with the color blue.

Be who you are, this is the gift. You are to be who you are. Let no one walk in your path but allow yourself to walk in yours and allow others to walk theirs. But if someone should come to block your path or to take you from it, that is the time for you to make the choice, to simply state, I AM THAT I AM, a Divine Inheritor, a Child of Creation. The work upon the planet is that of gathering of the Star Seed clusters. Many are confused, for there has long been interbreeding. You, yourself, suffer confusion, for you see, your body is intermingled and as you become clear in the Cellular Awakening, you are removing stones in your path. For the TIME IS NOW, for you to walk an uncluttered path, for you to remove these stones, for you to walk clearly in your being. You are to be who you are and allow no one to interfere with that.

This is the principle of strength. Call for this strength to be who you are and allow others to be who they are. This is the time that you do become the spiritual warrior. But who are you the warrior for, but for your path. You become, not the warrior against your Brother, you become the warrior for yourself. It is important for you to allow all to be who they are. And it is important for you to become individualized in your path of being. There is the saying that many are called, but few respond. There is much truth in this statement and strength, above all, is important. Strength, Dear hearts. I send you my love and blessings.

16

The Cellular Awakening initiates Ascension,
and the Violet Flame assists the Ascension process.

Transformation
Saint Germain

The golden summertime of the Pacific Northwest—the last days of July and the first weeks of August—has finally arrived. I escape for a week to the family cabin on Pend Oreille Lake in northern Idaho. Our daily trips to the beach and swimming in the Snake River are certainly magical, and our time spent at the lake will become a cherished memory that is affectionately evoked by the children during the long, cold winter months.

I've just unloaded the last of the groceries from my car when the phone rings. It's Sherry. "You need to come home. You have visitors and they are traveling here from out of state just to meet you." I adamantly tell Sherry that there is no way that will happen and that the children have looked forward to this trip for months.

We spend the next two days splashing in the cool water, diving and jumping off of the dock, and stuffing ourselves with huckleberry pancakes in the morning. There are afternoon picnics at the water's edge and evening barbeques ending with gooey smores in the translucent moonlight.

On the third day of our vacation the phone rings again, "You just have to come home, and come home as soon as possible. They'll be here tomorrow!" Sherry pleads.

I sense the urgency in her voice. After I hang up, my sister hears the stress in my voice as I express my dilemma. "I'll watch the kids for a night . . . you'd better go home and take care of business," she tells me.

I arrive in time for the trance-session, close to 5 p.m. I open Sherry's front door and in her living room is her husband, Steve, lying on a massage table, and a young man is obviously working on his aura—his light-fields—through a form of energy-work.

Sherry sits at her kitchen table with her tarot cards spread out. Sitting on the other side of the table is a distressed young woman. "I don't think this relationship is going to last long . . ." says Sherry.

I turn away, sensing their need for privacy.

The young man working with Steve notices me standing there, and he turns around and greets me with a generous, warm smile and shakes my hand, "Hi, I'm Len."

This man—his eyes, his smile; yes, I've known him before. It feels like the moment when I first gazed upon the portrait of Saint Germain.

"Would you walk with me for a minute?" says Len, gesturing toward the door. "I'm sure they'll be awhile," and he motions toward Sherry and the young woman. "I've just finished the energy balancing on Steve."

I glance at Steve; he is snoring.

"Okay," I say, and we walk together toward the park several blocks away. As we head for the beach, Len unabashedly locks arms with me. Normally I would never allow a perfect stranger to do this, but I have a peculiar, yet profound trust for this person.

We sit together on the grassy edge of the river's shore for what seems like an eternity, yet it was only twenty minutes. And in that time we become acquainted, or more accurately, re-acquainted.

Len hails from West Chester, Pennsylvania, and explains that he has made his trip out west via the Teton Mountains in Jackson Hole, on a spiritual quest. He speaks lovingly about his two children and mentions that he's single. I ask what he does for a living, and he tells me he originally pursued music and voice, and after obtaining a degree in music education, he'd taught for a short time, but by profession he's a building contractor. Could this be the teacher Sherry's Tarot Cards had prophesied?

I flash back to one of my final days with Dan. We had spread out the Medicine Cards. I had been crying and Dan was trying to offer me some sort of comfort and reminded me that some day the "right," person would again be in my life. My shaking hand had drawn the wolf—the consummate teacher. The image of Dan's face fades into this athletic, young man, now sitting by my side at the water's edge.

There is an intense, yet tender realization that Len and I have a connection beyond the physical restraints of time and space, and I feel Angels and nature Devas dancing about us on the green grass. I force myself to look at my watch, "We have to get back."

We walk to Sherry's house in silence, a little disappointed that our short time together has ended so soon. On the front porch, before we enter the house, Len grabs my hand and holds it to his heart. "When everything is said and done, all that is left is . . ." He pauses and before I can think or even blush, I finish his sentence: "Love?"

I'm a bit embarrassed as we each take a chair at the kitchen table and Sherry quickly finds her notepad with her questions. "It is important to know that before the channeling that the Spiritual Teachers will ask your permission to participate in the trance-session," Sherry explains. "And if you don't say okay, they won't start." Sherry lights up a cigarette and places it in the ashtray. I am so nervous, I almost light one up too.

Yet, I quickly and readily enter the trance state, and Saint Germain presents teachings on consciousness, Ascension, and more ongoing insight on the Cellular Awakening. However, just before the session ends, the same Angels and Devas who appeared with us on the beach join our circle, and a glowing Angel of light passes a cup for each of us to drink from. As I open my eyes from the dreamy state, I note that only Len and I can actually see the Angel's ethereal approach. Len places his hands around the golden goblet and drinks.

Welcome, my Beloveds, I AM Saint Germain. I AM most happy to be with you for discourse and am thankful that you request my opinion. As you have known through past discourses, it is through your freewill that we are allowed to contact you. Do we have your approval for such?

Response: "Yes."

We are most thankful to send our radiance and blessings to you and remind you of the use of the Pink Ray on the planet at this time. For it is Divine Compassion and Divine Love that mankind truly must integrate within his will and the Blue Ray of Truth. You see, it is the combination of the two which form the transformation upon the Earth Plane and Planet at this time.

In understanding the process of planetary transition, one must also understand the process of personal transformation. You are well aware of the collective consciousness and its effect upon the Earth Plane and Planet at this time. However, we would like to give you discourse on the influence of the Earth and her influence on collective consciousness, upon your body, upon your soul, and upon your mental body. It is important for you to understand that the planet, too, resonates with vibration and Divine Intelligence. This Divine Intelligence also acts and reacts to your actions and reactions. Beloveds, you have long felt too responsible for the reaction of the Earth. Do you not see that she too carries vibration, that she too carries her Divine Consciousness? This has an effect upon you. It is most important that you learn through the mental states of action versus reaction, that which brings you to the state of inner peace. Do you understand?

Response: "Yes."

This is the purpose of the Energy Vortices we have outlined to you in the map of upcoming Earth Changes. These Vortices are the synthesis of action and reactionary states of the Earth Planet as Divine Consciousness. You may perceive them as nerve endings. However, they are more than that. They contain within themselves, the synthesis of energy, that mankind may go to purify his own body, where he may go to be and to become ONE with the Source. Do you not see, Dear hearts, contained within the center of the Earth is Divine Consciousness. The Vortex areas are the locations where this Divine Consciousness is allowed to flow through in a more direct stream, as you may understand it. And so you see, Dear ones, in these locations are the more pure forms of her collective state.

Do you not see how your body perceives? You have energy points that exist upon your body, Chakra Centers, as you have known them. You also have sensory organs; you have the eyes, the ears, and the nose. Look to the planet in the same way. See these Vortices and see how they, too, are sensory organs. They are the sensory points that exist for her. My Beloveds, you have questions?

Question: "We wanted to make a movie presentation of your words about the Earth Changes. Would it be all right to show the devastation that is going to happen, in order to awaken people to listen? Would this be all right, as long as we also show the hope? How would you like us to present this?"

My Dear ones, it appears the devastation has never affected mankind, for have you not already blown yourself up with bombs? Have you not already done this devastation? Remember, Dear ones, this is a cleansing, this is a purification. It is being brought forth for such. It is a transition which purifies, cleanses, and heals not only the organism, the collective consciousness known as Earth or Terra but also that of your bodies. However, in addressing your question, we would be most delighted to guide and assist you.

We find it very important that you are able to share with as many as possible and ask that you do carry the message of hope and peace. For this, too, is our message, that the physical body will soon no longer be needed for expression. You see, Dear ones, you are indeed Divine Inheritors, not only of this garden from which you sprang but Divine Inheritors of eternal wisdom, eternal love, and eternal power. It is our hope, that through this transmission, that people will grasp this message. It is important to focus upon the use and acknowledgement of the Higher Self, the I AM Presence, guiding and directing you with your freewill as a Co-creative force with this Presence. Have I answered your questions?

Question: "Yes. Will our bodies also be changed at that time?"

Your bodies are changing at the present moment. You see, Dear one, you are now accelerating at a rate of .283 as compared to the beginning of the planetary transition. This is in direct alignment and correspondence, as well, to the collective consciousness of the planet. Do you understand, Dear one? You are in the process of Ascension. You are continuing this path day by day. To explain this process of Ascension, it is not a process that occurs over night but it is a process that occurs continually. Have you not sensed your needs have changed or shifted?

Response: "Yes."

You see, to compare this to a year ago, do you not see a major growth within yourself?

Response: "Totally."

It is the recognition of this process, so that we understand Ascension. You are ascending, Dear ones. Come forth and let your light shine. Come forth and demand, "I AM a Divine Inheritor, I AM a Child of the Garden, I AM come that I AM THAT I AM." Do you not see that this message is brought forth to uplift mankind? This message is brought forth for you to gain eternal love, wisdom, and power, that which you have fallen away from. However, as you are through the Cellular Awakening and now are forced to awaken to what you truly are and truly are to become, again there is the matter of freewill which enters into this message.

And there is much to be said over the freewill of mankind. However, as you learn, like a mathematical calculation or a scientific formula, through the right use of your will as a Co-creative force with God, the I AM Presence is the focus within your life. Do you not see?

Question: "Yes, I see that. There is one here who would like your guidance with the project of taping this work."

We are delighted to serve those who openly give their hand in service with us. Take our hand, my Dear Brother, and feel our Presence around you. We ask for you to use the Violet Flame at all times. Are you familiar with the use of the transmuting Flame of Mercy and Forgiveness?

Response: "Yes."

Beloved, we are most honored to serve you. The Violet Flame has been brought forth for mankind, for upliftment. You see, it is acceptance of the Violet Flame, Mercy, and Forgiveness, which brings upon the planet and upon your being the state known as Grace. There is much that has been said about this state of Grace. Grace is the peace which passes all things. However, Grace does not occur without Mercy and Forgiveness. And so, this Violet Flame has been brought forth.

I speak to you in mental concepts, so that you may understand. As you call forth through the spoken word, for the arrangement of the cells within your body, that which you know as the Aura, the energy force around your being, as you call out for its perfection, say "I AM the Violet Flame, I AM Mercy, I AM Forgiveness, I AM Divine Compassion, I AM the Violet Flame, I AM Perfection, I AM ONE with Peace, I AM the Violet Flame, I AM Mercy and Forgiveness, I AM Transformed, I AM THAT I AM. You see, Beloveds, as you call forth the transmuting flame, the eternal transmuting flame comes forth within your being and grants you forgiveness of the past, forgiveness of the future, and places you as one with the timeless present. This is what we have called the Cellular Awakening. Do you understand, my Dear one?

Response: "Yes."

I AM most happy to assist you and will also call forth for Archangel Michael to come with his brilliant Blue Flame, to guide you at all times, to keep you ever steady, ever faithful in the truth. For you see, Dear ones, the Light of God Never Fails. This is by far the highest decree you may send out into the universe. In discussing the topic of Earth Changes with the masses, it is most important, that you do not instill the human emotion of fear. It is most important that you instill peace and hope. There is a hand that guides and directs them at all times. There is a choice that can be made through the freewill to become ONE again with self.

Response: "We thank you."

I raise this Cup to you and ask for you to sup with me. I bring it forth in brilliance and radiance from the Spiritual Hierarchy. We are delighted to serve you.

There were six or seven beings here. There was one being who was here from another Solar System and he carried with him a crown and they followed him, walking quietly, one at a time.

17

*Relationships reflect back to us our own state of consciousness,
and contain the sacred contracts of the soul.*

Relationships

Saint Germain
Kuan Yin
Mary
Paul
Soltec

The next morning before Len leaves, he gives me his phone number and asks,
"Will you meditate with me at 6 a.m. every morning?" "Of course," I respond. And
I ask him, "Will you return?"

He looks at me with piercing grey eyes and affirms, "Yes."

Yet, I am still haunted by Dan. I wonder what he'll think if I'm with Len, and even
more concerning, what if we work together and operate I AM America? In order to
keep my thoughts lucid, I write all my concerns in a note to myself and call Dan.
"Will you meet with me?" I ask.

I haven't seen him for well over six weeks, and when he walks up to the park
table, he looks a bit thin, and not himself. He sits down, and I realize I'm anxious!
I pull out my list, and instead of being a loving compassionate friend, I interrogate:
"Why did you leave? Why did you say this? Do you realize I am all alone now?" I'm
nothing short of accusatory, and then I notice tears welling up in his eyes.

I feel shame and intense humiliation at my behavior. Yet inside the questions keep
swirling: "Why can't I detach? Why am I not growing?" And the worst, "Why am I
not evolving?"

As Dan walks away, I can't even apologize, and when I think about offering at least
a small, "I'm sorry," a deep, oozing anger overtakes me.

I ask Sherry the same questions as she shuffles and lays out the tarot cards. It's clear that these answers would not be found in one reading. She lays the deck down and speaks directly and firmly: "You're mad at men—period. You've carried this burden for many lifetimes, and now you need to let it go. In fact, if you want love in your life—real love—you need to make changes." The shaman has spoken.

Next week David arrives to spend five days with me and the children. He's been pushing me to make a commitment and has suggested that he could buy a home for me and the children. But something deep inside of me has resisted his kind and generous offer. During his visit, I decide that I need to diligently meditate and begin to use quantum amounts of the Violet Flame. The change I so desperately seek is indeed within.

In this session, Kuan Yin addresses the difficulties we encounter in relationships—most often between parent and child, and with committed partners—and how these "sacred contracts" mirror self and help us to individually cleanse past karmas and experience love—not only as emotion, but a higher love that reflects our conscious choice through our actions. Saint Germain also shares enlightening information on our most intimate relationship: our relationship with Source.

Welcome, my Beloved chelas, I AM Saint Germain. I AM delighted to greet you this evening and for your benefit, we bring Beloved Sister Kuan Yin, Beloved Mary, Beloved Paul, and our comrade, Beloved Soltec. We are here for your assistance and as we have in past discourse, ask for your permission to participate. For you must understand, we are not allowed to infringe upon your freewill and ask for your permission. Do we have such?

Response: "Yes."

I AM most delighted to be here and bring you my message of joy and peace. For you see, Dear ones, this is another lesson in this great experiment that you call life. It is joy. There is much joy in living here upon the planet, the Earth Plane, as you have called it. For you see, life is indeed a joy, it is to be experienced with much thankfulness and much joy for being here. We understand that there are times that you forget, the human is one who is constantly judging. It is almost impossible for you to be one in embodiment without judging. But as you move in and through the elements of judgment, we ask that you stand back to be, to give thanks, and to be at ONE with joy. I would like to introduce Beloved Kuan Yin.

Greetings, my Beloved Sisters of the Flame. I AM Kuan Yin. I have come to give you the message of compassion for the Earth Plane. See before you the red rose, that which is ONE with the universe. See before you, the Pink Flame, that which beats within the heart of man. See before you, the Golden Ray, come to enlighten you to this Fourth Plane. I AM most willing and joyful to answer your questions, for I bring to you the message of compassion for your Brother. As you move through judgment, remember this: to see what you see in your Brother, that which you have indeed within yourself.

Question: "I would like to know about relationships, especially between a child and a parent, how to handle a child's rebellion?"

The rebellious child has asked the parent to bring forth that which needs to be revealed. You see, it is the perception of rebellion and this perception of rebellion is what is to be revealed. You must understand the ties that exist between the parent and the child. There are ties that exist before entering into embodiment. There are also the ties that exist as the child enters into embodiment. In the case of the rebelling child, does not the rebelling child serve as the great mirror for the sponsor? And does not the sponsor serve as the great mirror for the child? However, we should like to impress upon you, the contract that is signed between the sponsor and the child. The sponsor is brought forth to guide and to nurture this child up to eighteen years of age. We should like to stress that up to the age of nine years of age, the child is liable under contract. The first nine years, the parent and the child implement this contract to its fullest extreme. And the second nine years, the child is allowed more freedom within the contract. However, we must stress the responsibility to carry forth the agreement to do such.

Question: "A lot of relationships seem to be in turmoil at this time. Could you help us with married relationships? Should we stay with relationships when we're not happy or should we leave? What's being asked of us?"

We have asked, above all, for one to love one another, to have compassion for the one we have selected as our mate, to understand how they too mirror ourselves back to ourselves. You may select a mate who is a clear mirror for you. You must understand, Dear ones, there are those who mirror so clearly back to yourself and there are those who merely stand side by side, in reciprocal relationship to you.

There is also that which we have referred to as the Time Compaction and there are many relationships that you need to close, prior relationships from what you have known as past embodiments. But as you will come to understand, there is no past or future, there is just the present moment. You have asked, "should this relationship end?" Do you not understand, it is ongoing and always will be.

Question: "So unless you work through it and learn to love this person, it will be an unhappy relationship until you learn to make it different, in this life or in other lives?"

We are saying that all relationships are founded on one principle and that is love. However, as we have taught in past discourse, that love is truly not an emotion; love is the choice that you make for peace through your actions. Do you not see that as you make this choice for peace that you are in lovingness for one another? Your relationships never end when you act in such a manner. They are in a continuum of the process of externalization of your internal peace.

Question: "One here would like to know if it is possible for her to find another job?"

She is stepping back and Mary steps forward.

My Children of the Flame, I AM most pleased to be with you this evening and am happy to participate in discourse with you. Beloved Children, we are so thankful for the work you do upon the Earth Plane and Planet and we are so happy that you nurture this work and hold it in your heart. I AM available for your questions, Dear ones.

Question: "Mary, there are people who are unhappy in their work but are afraid that there may not be other work for them. Can you help us?"

There is such strife upon the planet, there are so many who are unhappy in that which they would perceive as mundane. However, there are the forces that guide and direct us. It speaks within our heart. This is the concept of the Holy Spirit. It is available at all times for you to call upon, to open those doors and pathways to create happiness and joy in your life and in all that you do. Do you not see this?

Question: "Yes. I would like to ask about shamanism and how it fits with my life."

We have spoken of the twelve soul clusters, twelve soul groups. This is an offshoot of the eighth tribe. It is again, the practice of principles that we call for, to not be caught in mysticism and that which you have called magic. But we ask for you to practice with a pure, clean heart. This is the principle. This that you speak, of the eighth tribe, are the traditions that have been brought through the Bahashi, a great tribe which inhabited the Earth during the pre-Atlantean waves. It is to be seen clearly for the principle that it is.

Question: "Thank you. I would like to ask if there is a natural product to replace the hormones in our body, or to help our hormones."

There is indeed an enzyme that comes from the milk of the nursing cow.

Question: "I am familiar with that. Thank you. I have some. I would like to ask about how the ozone layer is affecting the Earth?"

As you observe this great womb that has brought you forth and suckled and nursed you, brought you up, your bodies to house your Spirit, do you see this planet this way too? Her shell that is around her, this that you call the ozone, is similar to what you call your light field or Auric Field. You suffer rips and tears also within your Auric Field, that of the feminine principle, the Mother that has sponsored you. We have talked much of the Chakra or energy centers. Do you see this?

Question: "Is it directly related to our mass consciousness, the rips and tears in our Auric Field?"

It is directed to hers specifically.

Question: "As we work on repairing our Auric Fields, will hers mend?"

"As above, so below." And indeed, I say to you, are you not part of her and she part of you. Are you not her child as you are a child of the Source?"

Saint Germain steps forward.

I AM here to continue this discourse with you. As usual, we ask for permission. I AM most thankful to be with you this evening and have enjoyed listening to your comments. However, I would like to remind you that you are of one group. And that is, you are indeed a Child of God. You are the offspring of this creative force, you have been brought forth in perfection and you will return as such. Do you not see this? That you are indeed perfect and whole as you are. We ask for you to rejoice as ONE with the Source and we have said many times, that to gain the clear understanding of the Source is to walk your individualized path.

We have said "to be or not to be." Do you not see, it is up to you, through your freewill, to take this Source that has been given the great gift of life, this life that has been given to you, and to walk firmly in your individualized path? It is up to you to understand the use of the will, the use of love, the use of wisdom, the use of power. Do you not see that it is all, all of these combined that are all perceptions of God? For is not the Source, a creative catalyzing energy that steps forth, containing all of these aspects? We ask for you to experiment with these. We ask for you to then choose, to choose that which is easier for you to express of this creative Source. I welcome your questions.

Question: "You're saying that there is no sin, no right, no wrong, just to be is all that's expected and God learns through us?"

Remember the relationship. You have been created by this Source and you did not create this Source. However, you are in the image of this Source. I ask for you to experience the gifts of this Source. However, the path through human embodiment, and let me emphasize this, the path through human embodiment is the individualized Presence of God. Do you understand? You have within your true nature and your true being, that which was seeded deep within your soul at the point of Creation. You have chosen, through human embodiment, to bring this forth, to exemplify this work, to bring it forth in its full force. However, to learn such a quality entails the interaction of the qualities of others. For what is love without love and what is love without wisdom? Do you understand?

Question: "I think so. I'm still confused about a lot of people saying if you did certain things, you'd go to hell. There are a lot of church concepts about things being wrong."

Would Creation create that to destroy itself? It is not so.

Question: "Is there such a thing as an evil spirit?"

There were in history, in periods of history of human embodiment, those known as tricksters in the astral realm. They have come forth to do that which they do. However, we would like to remind you of the work of the human and the human mind, which you have.

18

As Time Compaction accelerates your spiritual growth,
work to eliminate struggle and strife from your life.
See that you are ONE with your Divine Plan and Divine Blueprint.

Transitional Events

Sananda
Kuthumi
Saint Germain

Many of the trance sessions are also attended by Lynne and Glenda—and Saint Germain affectionately calls our group the *Sisters of the Flame*. One night I enter Sherry's house, and there is Lynne's sister, Julie. I am a bit surprised, especially since she is someone who is completely unexposed to this type of work and yet she's willing to sit for the session with acceptance and open-mindedness. The Spiritual Teachers must already understand that her spiritual level of development is receptive and Sananda welcomes her and performs an energetic healing, clearing both her heart and throat chakras.

Sherry asks a variety of questions in this session, ranging from those about Bigfoot to the purpose of animals as pets. The teaching evolves to insights on diet and the controversial stance of the Spiritual Teachers who advocate a vegan to vegetarian diet to cultivate spiritual development and accelerate Cellular Awakening. I've noticed that this diet does indeed help, and I have temporarily eliminated red meats and chicken. This creates yet another shift for me, and I readily notice that I can more clearly communicate with beings of both Fourth and Fifth Dimension.

Interestingly, at the end of this lesson, Saint Germain shares more provocative information regarding churches and the Anti-Christ! I must admit that I don't believe everything that the Spiritual Teachers say. I am, however, an advocate of their own important statement to "Take everything we say unto laboratory of self." And in this ever-changing spiritual landscape, even further incited by Time Compaction, I think we must always endeavor to remain practical and grounded.

Welcome, my Beloved Sisters, I AM Sananda. This evening, I AM here to bring you discourse on transitional events, for we have spoken of the Period of Transition. As we enter into this Time of Cleansing and Purification of the Earth Plane and Planet, you have entered into what you have been told, as a period of Time Compaction. I AM most happy to be with you, my beloved Sisters, and ask that you sup with me, for as I have said, the feast is prepared, the banquet is in front of you. Choose what you will from this great feast, for there is much that is brought to you. Many gifts are being brought at this time. As you have been faced with your tears, you have also been faced with that which you need to resolve within your affairs. For you see, you have been called to get your house in order. However, I would like to remind you, Dear ones, that there are, too, the great gifts that are being offered to you. I bring to you the Cup and ask that you drink with me. Again, before we enter into discourse, I must ask for your permission to enter your light field. Is this possible, Dear ones?

Response: "Yes."

I AM most happy to serve you and am here to answer your questions, my Beloveds.

Question: "Sananda, a lot of people are experiencing crazy emotions. Our government is behaving strangely. Other countries are doing strange things. Everything seems to be happening very fast. Is there a plan in process for these governments?"

There have been many who have gone inside the government at this time, who have the message within their heart and are doing much to bring about change internally. Their path is a long one indeed and there are many struggles in front of them. There are those who have chosen to abandon this way of being. However, as I have said before, "When in Rome." It is most important for you to eliminate struggle and strife from your life, to find the path of least resistance. For you see, Dear ones, this is also the path of enlightenment. However, we see your need for structure and organization, as your country grows with its needs of government. What are the true needs? What are the true wants? It is that of spiritual freedom. It is also that of spiritual power. For you see, one clearly cannot come from a source of inner being, without that of being empowered by that of spirit. And so, you each have within you the Christ Consciousness, ready to emerge, ready to come into full bloom, as we have spoken through the Cellular Awakening.

There is much strife and struggle in your governments at this time across the planet. There is much we see that has happened through genetic coding, through struggle and strife, for this is indeed the struggle and strife of the ego state. However, as one becomes acquainted with that which is the true self, that which rises above the ego state, which no longer serves mankind at this point in his development, one will realize that this can be removed effortlessly. There are those who work in the inner government. You must trust that we have selected these people to perform their function and we also ask for you to send your prayers and light and love to those who have served in this capacity, for it is not an easy path.

Question: "Thank you, Sananda. I was quite ill last year with a double respiratory infection and I'm in the process of working to cure it. Can you help me with this?"

My Dear one, it is a functioning of your Heart Chakra Center.

He would like for you to face him. Sananda is projecting energies through the center of his palms towards the person asking questions.

My Dear Child, it is most important that you love yourself.

He has just aligned your Heart Chakra with your Throat Chakra.

It is most important, my Dear one, that you speak that which comes forth from your heart. It is also most important that you accept those in your path that do not understand your higher path. May I assist you further?

Response: "I believe that one of the most difficult things for us is to love ourselves."

It is most important, my Dear one, that you see your body as an extension of the lovely Spirit that you are. It is most important that you see that your body has been brought forth to express this Divine Spirit that you truly are. Each cell within your being is a densified form of your spiritual self. You have been brought forth into this Earth Plane with great beauty and a great inner desire to express this upon the Earth Plane and Planet. Dear Child, remember that we are with you at all times and you are loved and wanted. It is most important that you understand that you serve a role and a significant role on the Earth Plane and Planet at this time. It is by no chance that you are here. You are here by what they call a Divine Appointment. We are most happy you are here and extend our hand in service to you.

My Dear one, accept a given situation. The acceptance of this situation allows this to move through the emotional body. For you see, it is the emotional body that is most closely associated with that of the physical body. The mental body lies between the spiritual body and the emotional body. It is important to accept a situation and then to release this through prayer and use of the Violet Flame, for Mercy and Forgiveness are Divine Qualities.

Question: "I would like to now ask about the creature known as Bigfoot. Where do they live? In the center of the Earth or do they live on the surface?"

They live upon the surface of the planet. However, they are plantings and are sparse and few between. Their genetic origin is from a race of beings which no longer exist upon your planet. This seed group has left a few, their harvest completed with the Fourth Manu. There are those who have remained who understand this information and collectively made the decision during the removal of the fourth Manu to stay upon the planet to tell the story and the history of their people, which existed before humankind.

Question: "Will there come a time when we will make contact with them so that they can tell us their history? Or are they too shy?"

My Dear one, they are not shy, but they are guarded. They simply understand that there is that which cannot be thrown before the swine.

Question: "Could I ask what function animals serve, like pets, in our life?"

I would like to address this question, however my beloved Brother Kuthumi is well versed in this and I ask for his intercession.

My beloved Brothers and Sisters, I welcome you. I AM Kuthumi. I have been brought forth on the Green Ray of Ministry to the Planet and Mankind, brought forth through the Elemental Life Force. I AM most happy to address your question. You see, animals are an extension of Elemental Life Force, brought forth through the mental plane of mankind, combined with the Elemental Life Force of earth, air, and water. However, the Divine Spark of Creation has not existed within animals at this time. It is brought forth through the Divine Spark of the mental plane, manifested through human thought. For you see, Dear ones, animals have been created for use upon the planet for man, were brought forth to be his companions, his comforters, those that have been brought forth to soothe him through his embodiment. Do you understand?

Question: "Are they able to bring balance to people?"

They are the grand soothers. They have been brought forth to soothe you. You see, Dear ones, you have learned much through animals upon the planet. You have seen them giving of themselves unconditionally over and over, is this not so? What a great lesson this has been for mankind to see. And it is a great service that they have performed, for you see, they function with a collective consciousness. That is what they are able to tap into, that which has been created through the collective consciousness of the mental plane. It has been decided at the levels of Hierarchy that each gene pool will be allowed the Divine Spark.

Question: "So animals will receive that?"

Each gene pool will come forth collectively to receive the Divine Spark.

Question: "Is it not true that animals show us how to love, truly love?"

You see, Dear ones, love is not an emotion. Love is a doing and a being. Is this not what you have seen in your great friends that you call animals?

Question: "Is there any retribution if people harm animals?"

You see, Dear one, there is not. This is difficult for you to understand. For you see, it functions upon the mental plane, created for mankind to move through his many lessons. This is quite difficult for you to comprehend when you see a person who is quite cruel to animals on the planet. However, these Elemental Forces have offered themselves in service to do this for mankind and it has been decided, as I have stated before, at the Hierarchical Level, that these entities that have sponsored themselves, given so much in service of their Divine Energies, be offered the Creative Spark.

Question: "What is the difference between the domestic cattle and the wild deer or elk?"

Domestic animals are more closely classified and qualified with human emotions. You see, Dear ones, as they enter into the close mental field near the human emotion, those which you have known to be domesticated for your planet, particularly the cow, have a developed an emotional body and field.

Response: "That doesn't feel very good, that people could eat an animal with an emotional body."

You must understand, Dear ones, this is why we have called a halt of animal product usage in dietary standards upon the planet. For you see, it is the emotional field that remains qualified within the body itself and we ask that you do not take this upon yourself. Do you understand?

Question: "Yes. How about fish? Is that considered the same?"

That which has not absorbed the emotional qualities quite so densely is an easier form of vibratory action to take into your system. However, we ask that you no longer take animal products of any kind into your system.

Question: "And that includes eggs and milk?"

That would include all animal products. For you see, Dear ones, we are asking for you to become ONE with your Divine Plan and Blueprint. There is much confusion that occurs as you take on the emotional body, not only that of the animal, but it has absorbed much from many it has encountered in its presence upon the Earth Plane and Planet. We ask for you to walk truly within the light of your true being and Divine Plan and that will assist in your Cellular Awakening.

Question: "Then eating more green vegetables would be the way to bring that about?"

My Dear one, it is our hope to bring forth the technologies that will greatly assist you in finding new foodstuffs to assist you in Fourth Dimension vibration.

Question: "Could you explain more about Time Compaction?"

My beloveds, I would like to introduce you to my comrade and coworker, Saint Germain.

Welcome, my beloved chelas, I AM Saint Germain. I AM most happy to be with you this evening. I will address your question on Time Compaction. You see, Dear ones; there was acceleration upon the Earth Plane. Have you not felt this? You see, we are most happy with the development and the acceptance of the Cellular Awakening upon the planet at this time. And we, at the cosmic levels, have called forth through your cries for peace, Time Compaction. It is being ushered in through not only the wind element but that of the fire element. You see, Dear ones, it is the wind element that carries the cosmic rays to your being.

[*Editor's Note:* It is important to note that when using theories of Time Compaction, the Masters are referring to personal transition, planetary transition, and transition of the collective consciousness. It is apparent that we are in a period of Grace, where we can personally accelerate our energetic bodies to Fourth Dimension. It also appears, as more of us achieve this, a collective momentum is created, as occurred in the One Hundredth Monkey Theory. This dynamic of Time Compaction helps to create more accessibility to Fourth Dimension and the end result is the rise of mass collective consciousness. There are those who go first and hold space, so the way is clear for others. This is the differentiation of the individual path and the collective path and the path of the planet. The planet herself has an individual path. She is in transition, but at her own rhythm and this rhythm is her choice as a cosmic being of great consciousness, sound, and light.]

My beloved chelas, I would like to impress upon you the great joy that we feel. Do you not see and rejoice, that you are making in your development and soul memories at this time, the possibility that as you make each leap, you have the ability through Time Compaction theories, to double that which proceeds? We rejoice with you and are most happy for the continued service given upon the Earth Plane and Planet at this time.

However, there is that faction, which we would like to discuss with you, that which is the strife within your religious world. There has been much discussion of this at our levels and we ask for resolution of these upon the planet. There has been much control of information of our Plan and Purpose on the Earth Plane and Planet at this time that has been kept hidden from the general public.

Question: "By the churches?"

Yes. It is most important that this information be brought forth to the light, the Light of God that Never Fails.

Question: "Could you give us some idea of what this information is?"

This information will give you specific details, of not only Earth Change events, but of the exact times that we are allowed to enter back into the Earth Plane. You see, Dear ones, this is indeed the Divine Plan.

Question: "When they talk of the Second Coming, they talk of Christ coming back to Earth, to the churches specifically and being among them, is that what you're talking about?"

We are speaking specifically of the information in unadulterated form. You see, I have spoken to you of the twelve Star Seed families. And I assure you, Dear ones, there is much to be learned. It is most important that this information be brought out from the cloak of ignorance, brought out so that the public may learn and understand from it. It is not our intention to instill fear into the hearts of man. However, as we make our preparations, there are many who must become informed regarding this mission. Do you not see how this could be used against Hierarchical Purpose?

Response: "Yes."

This is the ego state functioning at its fullness. I ask for you to call forth Divine Wisdom. Call forth the Light of God that Never Fails. Call forth the Violet Flame, not only for yourself, but for this church group, so that the keys are given to unlock these secrets. For you see, Dear ones, I could give you this information; however, there is this information written in stone.

Question: "Where is this stone?"

This stone is held in Switzerland.

Question: "Is it translated?"

There is no need for translation.

Question: "And it gives precise dates of the Earth Changes?"

It gives precise dates.

Question: "If the Time Compaction can change and double as it has, does that mean the Earth Changes will pick up too?"

There is the possibility that this will happen.

19

Instead of swinging from one polarity to the next,
spiritual growth is an ever-expanding ascending spiral.

In the Image and Likeness

Saint Germain
Soltec
Mary

I have been invited to speak at the annual Global Sciences Congress in Denver. I admit, I am a little edgy. At this conference I will present the Map in front of hundreds of people. Even though I've become somewhat adept at presenting the slide show to ten to twenty people in small groups, this is totally different. Sherry assures me that I'll do just fine, as she is adamant that every time I get an opportunity to share this message, the Spiritual Teachers will guide and protect me. David promises that he will fly into Denver and support me at this lecture, but for some reason I feel uneasy about that. He is busy with work and his career, and something tells me that even though he wants to commit himself to me and the children, he is not ready.

The day before I leave, David calls to tell me that it is doubtful he will be able to attend. Glenda assures me that she will be there with me, and will support me through my lecture, and another member of our spiritual group—Priscilla, a grandmother and an elder of the Nez Perce tribe—will also attend my lecture. The day of the lecture, the phone rings in my hotel room and surprisingly it is Len. "I'm packing, I have bought my plane ticket, and I will be there for you." My heart beats with excitement, yet I also experience a calm centeredness, knowing that I will see him again.

As I step on the stage, I face over 200 people. To the left of the stage, both Glenda and Priscilla sit with pride and peaceful composure. I am aware that they are simultaneously calling in numerous Spiritual Teachers and feeding me vital spiritual energy. I also feel the undeniable love and support of friendship and the kinship of our Sisterhood. The host begins to ask me questions, and soon my jitters subside. Afterwards I am flooded with people, asking questions. Apparently they all want to meet and talk to the "Map Lady." My work with sharing the Map and its prophecies of change has suddenly spiraled to a new level.

This lesson was received one week before I left for Denver. In this selection, Saint Germain, Soltec, and Mary address this same metaphysical spiral that is present in our spiritual growth. This evolutionary spiral is the culmination of many spiritual tenets: right use of will, emotional discipline, forgiveness—both of self and for others, and, as always, oceans of Violet Flame. All of these practices help to create our shift into Fourth and Fifth Dimensional reality.

I did not know it at the time, but the following selection was to become my last session with the beloved "Sisters of the Flame." My life's trajectory would soon change, and I would quickly face a transformational juncture in the ascending spiral of my own spiritual path.

≈

[*Editor's Note:* This material had not been transcribed previously and was taken directly from the tape. Saint Germain's discourse was picked up mid-sentence with "the eight-sided and fourteen particle radiated substance is the collective energy force that is called I AM THAT I AM. . ." Though a bit out of context, this concept is important. *Points of Perception* contains Saint Germain's teaching of the Eight-Sided Cell of Perfection within our heart, as the Source within everyone. Focusing upon this Cell accelerates our return to perfection. Also, the light from this Cell spreads throughout our energy bodies—this cleanses and restores our spiritual light. The fourteen particles may have a connection to our seven lower and seven higher energy bodies.]

The eight-sided, fourteen particle radiated substance, which is the collective energy force called I AM THAT I AM, is at your beck and call. For you see, Dear ones, when you call on that which I AM, it is a direct alignment of the energy force. Do you not see this great harmony that exists between light and sound, corresponding one to the next? And where you call this into motion, knowing love as a choice, it is indeed the right use of your will and action, action being that of power, the highest principle of God. Do you understand, Dear ones, you are indeed God beings who have been put upon this planet to be responsible for your energy or power within, to balance love, wisdom, and power. Dear ones, do you see this to be your truth?

All respond: "Yes."

And so, Dear ones, I have been part lengthy, for I realize that you have many questions and I AM most willing to serve you, you Beloved Children.

Question: "Does emotion then block the right use of will?"

Emotion allows, in some instances, the world to come forth, for you see, there are particles within emotion itself that serve this will. It is indeed the right use of will that we speak about. It is emotion that has come indeed out of balance. Dear ones, we are not against emotion, for the e-motion is what we truly speak about. It is for the balance and harmony for the use of such. There are those that go, as we call it, quite overboard in their use of these faculties. You have an emotional body, which is part of your total make-up, energetic make-up or genetic make-up, whatever you wish to call it. Dear ones, are you not made in the image and likeness of God? For there are times that God's passion has brought one forth to a greater source of creativity. But yet, does He draw within the passion? No, Dear ones, He uses this to catapult into the Source of Creation. Do you understand?

Question: "Yes. When you are working with the emotional body and trying to cleanse it and purify it, isn't it a discipline?"

It is indeed a discipline. For as you see, as the pendulum swings, how difficult it is to keep it within the center. Have you not seen this pendulum swing back and forth through your many emotional experiences? It is a discipline to not become the pendulum that swings far to the left or far to the right. It is indeed a great work to stay within the middle, for you see that is where the Hand of God holds this pendulum straight and has access to all true creativity of the universe.

Question: "Then, isn't it also true there is both the horizontal and vertical in the swing, which in turn creates a cross? And isn't the vertical, the lifting of the energies on the Earth Plane to the higher levels?"

Dear Sister, you are correct in assuming that this cross exists and it is available for your choice to work within this cross. However, it is the circle that we are most concerned about. Have you not too observed that a pendulum not only goes horizontally and vertically but also within a circle of eternal Creation. It is the disciplined energy that knows which way to turn and to use this, which is available for use at all times. It is our recommendation that it is the circular motion that you focus and concentrate upon, for the circular motion comes to the point which is the spiral and the spiral is the point of Creation where one moves on. Instead of moving from left to right to right to left to up and down, do you not see how it is the circular motion that allows one to ascend in motion?

And this is my greatest teaching I would tell you upon this point, that it is important to remain in the circular motion, my Dear ones, at all times. This has been brought forth through the use of the Decree of the Violet Flame, the Law of Mercy, and Forgiveness. It allows one's energetic bodies, all fourteen bodies, to remain within the spiral motion. At times, you will see that these are very small steps or spirals, as you would call them; however, Dear ones, it is on the ascent.

Question: "Is it important for us to raise the energies from this level and receive energies from the higher levels to accomplish the work desired by the Masters?"

That which draws like to its like follows the eternal law that likes seek likes, seeking its own level. For you see, as one enters into the spiraling motion, there are thoughts of how it has gone before. This leaves, what you would call the electromagnetic trail that one may follow behind this stream, this wondrous stream of light energy, as you would call it. As you reach and ascend to it, it has broken a trail, as you would call it. In Quantum Physics, it is referred to as a mathematical formula known as .56/82. This that you follow upon, Dear ones, has broken this stream for you, a way for you to follow through.

Dear one, when you come into this spiral, that which is the Violet Flame spiral, you go where those have gone before you and reach to their energies. There is that which you have grabbed upon and pulled upon, the energy of an Ascended Master. However, has he not left this graciously for you to pull upon? For indeed, as you pull upon it and you merge, you collect these energies, then become separate entities. Do you understand?

Question: "Yes. There is a question from someone else who would like to know more about the high winds. Will they be blowing everywhere and what should we do?"

Dear one, to answer this question, I would like to call forth my Beloved Brother Soltec.

Welcome, my Beloved Sisters, I AM Soltec and as you shall become acquainted with me, I AM known upon the Green Ray in the Ministry of Service to Science and this question that you have addressed with Earth Change information, the violent winds that you will incur, are only really a matter of magnetic shift within the Earth Plane. This shift shall occur, because as you see, there is a direct relationship of the consciousness of mankind to that which occurs within the lower levels of the energy field of the Earth. And so, there are these shifts which are indeed to occur, for you see, Dear ones, there is this period of time which has long been prophesied within the Akashic Record of Earth Planet, that are known as a pattern that has been set forth by many before you. And so indeed, we have again the duplication of this pattern to come forth.

In reference to your question of what you may do. Yes indeed, these winds will be blowing all around the Earth Plane and Planet. There is much that you can do for your physical body. There is also much you can do for your other bodies, thirteen bodies to be exact. For you must understand, this is not only the monumental shift that has happened in Third Density or Third Dimension, as you understand it, but in the mental shift that has occurred in the higher energetic layers. There are three shifts that are to occur, each shift affecting four energetic layers at each time. And so you have the first shift and four energetic layers are affected. The second shift, another four. And the final shift, you go down to where the Third Density has finally been affected. Dear one, we have given instruction for you to go within the pyramidal structures that face within the new magnetic North, those which are structured to go underground within your Earth. These will be available for your use.

Question: "Would you tell us something about the structure of the economy after the Earth Changes?"

Dear one, I AM Soltec and I call forth the love of Saint Germain to continue facilitating.

Welcome, my Beloved Sisters, I AM Saint Germain and I will address the economic situation. As my Brother Sananda has said before, "this time is to come, the four pillars to shake," as we have spoken before of the families, the four families that have long ruled, for the last two thousand years, your economic systems. As we have indicated before, there is discord and disharmony within these families and the fifth one that is to enter will cause this to crumble. We have spoken about the millennium, the time that is to come, and the use of gold. For you see, Dear ones, it is the vibration that we are concerned about, that it should be circulated freely and free use of this metal be used. If you are concerned about your economy and your exchange of money, look at your exchange of energy. For is this not the representation of both? If you have, what you call, within your economy that which needs to be guarded, do so. We have long viewed the economy of the Earth Plane and it will soon change. May I assist you further?

Question: "I have been asked to go to Juneau, Alaska. Can you give me more information as to when and what will be my purpose for this trip?"

There is indeed that city if you would wish to go there. However, as I have stated before, your work is within the Gobean area, that which is to the North and to the East quadrant.

Question: "For what work and what purpose will I be in Gobean?'

My Dear one, you drank from the Cup that you would never forget. There are many who know so little about these teachings and are these not for the upliftment of mankind? And during this Time of Transition, are there not many who will be asking and thirsting to drink from this Cup as you have? Hand the Cup to them.

Question: "Do you have any further instructions to give to me regarding this Cup?"

Do your work with joy, Dear one, for is not this a joy to be on this planet at this time? Are you not honored to be here and to sit here, a member of this great Planetary Council? Hold you head high, Dear one, for you indeed carry the Light of God that Never Fails. It is a blessing to serve you, Dear ones and I would like to step back for a moment and turn the floor over to Beloved Mary.

My Dear ones, I come forth. I AM Mary and I bring change information for your area. For you see, Dear ones, this is indeed my area of focus, for this is where my life has begun and where I will begin to serve as we enter into the seventh dispensation and prepare for the Eighth Ray upon the Earth Plane and Planet known as Terra of the Christos. My Dear ones, be prepared for the winds that will come from the East and from the South, those that will be accompanied by the sheets of wind and rain. Be prepared for the lights that come throughout the sky, those that will come from the East and from the North. Be prepared for the rushing of water that will last for no less than six years throughout your area. And in all of this, Dear ones, remember the great joy of this great cleansing which has come forth. Remember this joy that has been patterned within your planet to set the frequency to receive that of Fourth Dimensional reality. Remember the Great Ones of Light that are coming, to be embodied, to be upon the planet during this period of one thousand years, those who come from the universes.

Saint Germain returns.

I AM most happy to continue this discourse with you. Again, I AM open and willing to serve you and await your questions.

Question: "Where did we come from before we came to this planet and perhaps you could give us some background?"

My Dear ones, as you have understood, the point of Creation is the Great Central Sun, that which is the Great Spark of Creation that comes forth as the center of your system of worlds. There is that which is known as the Celestial Kingdom or Celestial Universe. There is also that which is known as the Arcturian Universe, that which is known as the Murhananda Universe, that which is known as the Dahl Universe, that which known as the Pleiadian Universe, that which is known as the Leheiss Universe, that which is known as the Wehanno Universe. Dear ones, the orbit of these and the final Universe that was created is the Christos Universe.

Your origin, of course, is the point of Creation, that which is the Great Central Sun. However, you have had embodiments in that which is known as Arcturus, that which brought it seeds to the time upon the Christos known as Lemuria. There are also those among you who have spent time upon the great system known as the Pleiades. And there is one among you who is an ambassador from the Dahl. Dear ones, it is not so much your point of origin or your last point of origin but who you are in the present moment, that which is empowered from the great source of Creation, your mighty I AM Presence. Be that creative being that you are, made in the image and likeness of the great Alpha and Omega. Come forth in your majestic brilliance, the Love of Brother/Sister Flame.

Question: "When will be the best time to move to Gobean? And will I be guided once there?"

They ask for you to be prepared within the next four months, your move to be complete. You will know, Dear one, when you arrive, for you will be greeted by a grand sunset.

Question: "Is there any way that I could awaken my son to understanding more of what is going to happen?"

My Dear one, there was a parable that was taught by my Beloved Brother Sananda about the sower of the seed. He grabbed from his bag and threw the seed onto the ground. Some of it fell upon fertile ground, some upon the rocks; some was captured and taken by the birds. You have sewn many seeds within your son but it is his responsibility of how this is to grow and the nature of his soil. Do you not see, Dear one, you may help him tend his garden. You may help the many plants that grow within his soul. But there is that which is his as well. Have you not raised your son? Do you not continue to throw the seed upon his ground? Do not worry, Dear one, there is that which is the timed orderliness of the universe, that which you have known as predestination, that which was determined long ago. Do not worry about your son, Dear one.

Question: "Could you tell us more about the Fourth Dimension?"

The Fourth Dimension is an alignment area where the physical and the spiritual meet and merge as ONE, and total alignment of all nine Chakras occurs. We ask, in the higher levels of Third Density, for the alignment of at least Seven Chakras before you enter into what is known as Four. In this Fourth Dimension, you will learn the alignment of the eighth and ninth Chakras and energetic bodies, to allow you to come into full manifestation. Do you understand, Dear one, there are those among you who have walked upon your planet, who have functioned within this dimension. Yes, they too carry the energetic pattern to be visible to your naked, physical eye. However, they come forth with much enlightenment, for they too have cleared the sub-atomic particles which rotate and spin on the Golden Thread Axis.

Beloveds, as I have stated before, it is the use of the Violet Flame which brings forth this alignment of Seven Chakra Centers. Three times a day, I have asked of you, three times to use the Flame of Mercy and Forgiveness. Not for others am I speaking of this, for this Forgiveness and Mercy starts within. For, as you well know, is it not that which is contained within yourself, which you may send to your neighbor and Brother? You must hold the gift within before you may give it away.

My Dear Sisters, I will take my leave from you now and offer you the Cup as you gather. Remember who I AM and, above all, never forget who you are. Bless you one and all, I AM.

Spiritual Lineage of the Violet Flame

The teachings of the Violet Flame, as taught in the work of I AM America, come through the Goddess of Compassion and Mercy Kuan Yin. She holds the feminine aspects of the flame, which are Compassion, Mercy, Forgiveness, and Peace. Her work with the Violet Flame is well documented in the history of Ascended Master teachings, and it is said that the altar of the etheric Temple of Mercy holds the flame in a Lotus Cup. She became Saint Germain's teacher of the Sacred Fire in the inner realms, and he carried the masculine aspect of the flame into human activity through Purification, Alchemy, and Transmutation. One of the best means to attract the beneficent activities of the Violet Flame is through the use of decrees and invocation. However, you can meditate on the flame, visualize the flame, and receive its transmuting energies like "the light of a thousand suns," radiant and vibrant as the first day that the Elohim Arcturus and Diana drew it forth from our solar sun at the creation of the Earth. Whatever form, each time you use the Violet Flame, these two Master Teachers hold you in the loving arms of its action and power.

The following is an invocation for the Violet Flame to be used at sunrise or sunset. It is utilized while experiencing the visible change of night to day, and day to night. In fact, if you observe the horizon at these times, you will witness light transitioning from pinks to blues, and then a subtle violet strip adorning the sky. We have used this invocation for years in varying scenes and circumstances, overlooking lakes, rivers, mountaintops, deserts, and prairies; in huddled traffic and busy streets; with groups of students or sitting with a friend; but more commonly alone in our home or office, with a glint of soft light streaming from a window. The result is always the same: a calm, centering force of stillness. We call it the Space.

Invocation of the Violet Flame for Sunrise and Sunset
I invoke the Violet Flame to come forth in the name of I AM that I AM,
To the Creative Force of all the realms of all the Universes, the Alpha, the Omega, the Beginning, and the End,
To the Great Cosmic Beings and Torch Bearers of all the realms of all the Universes,
And the Brotherhoods and Sisterhoods of Breath, Sound, and Light, who honor this Violet Flame that comes forth from the Ray of Divine Love—the Pink Ray, and the Ray of Divine Will—the Blue Ray of all Eternal Truths.

I invoke the Violet Flame to come forth in the name of I AM that I AM!
Mighty Violet Flame, stream forth from the Heart of the Central Logos, the Mighty Great Central Sun! Stream in, through, and around me.

(Then insert other prayers and/or decrees for the Violet Flame.)

Glossary

Alpha-Omega: According to Ascended Master teachings, our solar sun is one of seven evolved suns from the lineage of Twelve Ancestral Suns. Alpha and Omega—our current Great Central Sun—is overseen by a larger ancestral sun, known in Ascended Master myth as the Mighty Elohae-Eloha. It is claimed that of the twelve great central suns, Alpha and Omega is the fourth; and from their lineage seven smaller suns evolve: the Seven Galactic Suns. The fourth sun of the Seven Galactic Suns is Helios and Vesta, Earth's sun.

America: America—Canada, the United States, Mexico, Central and South America—finds its meaning from the esoteric word "Ameru," which means, "Land of the Plumed Serpent." Some claim America is an anagram which means the, "I AM Race."

Alignment: Convergence or adjustment.

Astral Body or Plane: This subtle light body contains our feelings, desires, and emotions and exists as an intermediate light body between the physical body and the Causal Body (Mental Body). According to the Master Teachers, we enter the Astral Plane through our Astral Body when we sleep, and many dreams and visions are experiences in this Plane of vibrant color and sensation. Through spiritual development, the Astral Body strengthens, and the luminosity of its light is often detected in the physical plane. A spiritual adept may have the ability to consciously leave their physical body while traveling in their Astral Body. The Astral Body or Astral Plane has various levels of evolution and is the heavenly abode where the soul resides after the disintegration of the physical body. The Astral Body is also known to esoteric scholars as the Body Double, the Desire Body, and the Emotional Body.

Anaya: A Spiritual Master and Teacher from the Pleiades who assists in the comprehension of science and new technology. Anaya is associated with the Golden Beam, the Golden Ray, and humanity's spiritual movement into the consciousness of ONE.

Angelic Host: According to the Ascended Masters, seven unique Angels assist and protect each individual in their spiritual growth and evolution. This is referred to as the Angelic Host.

Archangels *(the Seven)*: The seven principal angels of creation are: Michael, the Blue Ray; Jophiel, the Yellow Ray; Chamuel, the Pink Ray; Gabriel, the White Ray; Raphael, the Green Ray; Uriel, the Ruby Ray; and Zadkiel, the Violet Ray.

Atlantis: An ancient civilization of Earth, whose mythological genesis was the last Puranic Dvapara Yuga—the Bronze Age of the Yugas, and its demise occurred around the year 9628 BC. The legends of Atlantis claim the great empire co-existed with Ameru, Lemuria, and the Lands of Rama. According to Theosophical thought, Atlantis's evolving humanity brought about an evolutionary epoch of the Pink Ray on the Earth, and the development of the Astral-Emotional bodies and the Heart Chakra. Ascended Master provenance claims the Els—now the Mighty Elohim of the Seven Rays—were the original Master Teachers to the spiritual seekers of Atlantis. Esoteric historians suggest three phases of political and geophysical boundaries best describe its ancient record: the Toltec Nation of Atlantis (Ameru); the Turian Nation of Atlantis (the invaders of the Land of Rama); and Poseid, the Island Nation of the present-day Atlantic Ocean. The early civilizations of Atlantis were ruled by the spiritually evolved Toltec and their spiritual teachings, ceremonies, and temples were dedicated to the worship of the sun. Atlantean culture later deteriorated into the use of nuclear weapons and cruelty towards other nations, including the use of genetic engineering. The demise of Atlantis was inevitable; however, modern-day geologists, archaeologists, and occultists all disagree to its factual timing. Ascended Master teachings affirm that Atlantis—a continent whose geophysical and political existence probably spanned well over 100,000 years—experienced several phases of traumatic Earth Change. This same belief is held by occult historians who allege the Earth repeatedly cycles through periods of massive Earth Change and cataclysmic pole-shifts that activate tectonic plates which subsequently submerge whole continents and create vital New Lands for Earth's successors.

Ascended Masters: Once an ordinary human, an Ascended Master has undergone a spiritual transformation over many lifetimes. He or she has Mastered the lower planes—mental, emotional, and physical—to unite with his or her God-Self or I AM Presence. An Ascended Master is freed from the wheel of Karma. He or she moves forward in spiritual evolution beyond this planet; however, an Ascended Master remains attentive to the spiritual well-being of humanity, inspiring and serving the Earth's spiritual growth and evolution.

Ascension: A process of Mastering thoughts, feelings, and actions that balance positive and negative Karmas. It allows entry to a higher state of consciousness and frees a person from the need to reincarnate on the lower Earthly planes or lokas of experience. Ascension is the process of spiritual liberation, also known as *moksha*.

Aura: The subtle energy field of luminous light that surrounds the human body.

Awakening Point: The Awakening Points facilitates the *Spiritual Awakening* and is contained in the evolving human energy system. It is the nexus of the prophesied eighth human Chakra, and exists three to four yards from both the Heart Chakra and the Crown Chakra. Since this forms a pyramid shape, its termination point is referred to as the "Eighth Triad."

Awakening Prayer: Ascended Masters Saint Germain and Kuthumi offered this prayer to more than 200 people at the 1990 Global Sciences Congress in Denver, Colorado. Group and individual meditation of the Awakening Prayer encourage a heightened spiritual consciousness and Cellular Awakening.

Great Light of Divine Wisdom,
Stream forth to my being,
And through your right use
Let me serve mankind and the planet.
Love, from the Heart of God,
Radiate my being with the presence of the Christ
That I walk the path of truth.
Great Source of Creation,
Empower my being,
My Brother,
My Sister,
And my planet with perfection,
As we collectively awaken as one cell.
I call forth the Cellular Awakening.
Let wisdom, love, and power stream forth to this cell,
This cell that we all share.
Great Spark of Creation, awaken the Divine Plan of Perfection.
So we may share the ONE perfected cell,
I AM.

Bahashi: A tribe of the eighth soul group family in Earth's esoteric history. The Bahashi Tribe is claimed to have existed prior to Atlantis and spiritually venerated the original practice of shamanism.

Blue Flame: The activity of the Blue Ray, based upon the activation of the individual will, manifests the qualities of truth, power, determination, and diligence in human endeavors.

Blue Ray: A Ray is a perceptible light and sound frequency, and the Blue Ray not only resonates with the color blue, but is identified with the qualities of steadiness, calm, perseverance, transformation, harmony, diligence, determination, austerity, protection, humility, truthfulness, and self-negation. It forms one-third of the Unfed Flame within the heart—the Blue Ray of God Power, which nourishes the spiritual unfoldment of the human into the HU-man (the God-Man). Use of the Violet Flame evokes the Blue Ray into action throughout the light bodies, where the Blue Ray clarifies intentions and assists the alignment of the Will.

Buitsha: The Fourth Dimension of the Logos Web of Creation. This plane of energy is known as the "Heart" of the life-giving grid.

Celestial Kingdom: The Kingdom of Angels including Seraphim, Cherubim, Thrones, Dominions, Virtues, Powers, Principalities, Archangels, and the Angelic Host including the Guardian Angel.

Cellular Awakening: A spiritual initiation activated by Master Teachers Saint Germain and Kuthumi. Through this process the physical body is accelerated at the cellular level, preparing consciousness to recognize and receive instruction from the Fourth Dimension.

Chakra(s): Sanskrit for wheel. Seven spinning wheels of human-bioenergy centers stacked from the base of the spine to top of the head.

Chakra System: The human energy system of the Seven Chakras, including the Kundalini. In Sanskrit, *Kundalini* literally means coiled, and represents the coiled energy located at the base of the spine, often established in the lower Base and Sacral Chakras. *Kundalini Shatki* (shatki means energy) is claimed to initiate spiritual development, wisdom, knowledge, and enlightenment.

Christ, the, *or* **Christ Consciousness:** The highest energy or frequency attainable on Earth. The Christ is a step-down transformer of the I AM energies, which enlighten, heal, and transform all human conditions of degradation and death.

Christos Universe: Earth is a member of this cluster of stars.

Christ Self: Christ Self, also known as the Higher Self or Guardian Angel, protects the physical body, even though it operates at a lower vibratory rate than the I AM Presence. It also provides an intermediary power between the I AM Presence and the outer human form. Simply speaking, this intelligent body of light serves the energies of the I AM as a Step-down Transformer and a propellant of action in the physical plane.

Collective Consciousness: The higher interactive structure of consciousness as *two or more.*

Consciousness: Awakening to one's own existence, sensations and cognitions.

Creative Spark, *also known as the Unfed Flame:* The three-fold flame of divinity that exists in the heart and becomes larger as it evolves. The three flames represent Love (pink); Wisdom (yellow); and Power (blue).

Crown Chakra: Known in Sanskrit as the *Sahasrara,* this Chakra is located at the top of or just atop of the head. This Chakra connects our human consciousness to the spiritual planes. The Crown Chakra, also known as the Seventh Chakra, is perhaps the most unique of the Seven Chakras as this is where the Seven Rays enter the Chakra System. In the Hindu system the Crown Chakra is also known as the Chakra of One-Thousand Petals.

Cup: The Ascended Masters often refer to our human body as a Cup filled with our thoughts and feelings; it is also a symbol of neutrality and grace.

DAHL Universe: A star cluster which is said to exist beyond the Pleiades Universe.

Deva: Shining one or being of light.

Divine Blueprint: This energy field of the Human Aura maps the major and minor Energy Meridians and the gross and subtle Nadis (energy currents) of the Human body. The Divine Blueprint is said to also hold the spiritual information of the Divine Plan for the individual lifetime.

Divine Compliment: The idea that the ONE creative spark of the soul's genesis divides into two distinct parts: one part female, the other part male. The twin aspects of the soul play a number of roles with each other throughout successive lifetimes, and as the soul evolves and spiritually grows, this interaction perfects and expands. This same concept is known as Twin Flames; however the term Divine Compliment specifically describes the twin aspects of the soul as it exists in the Fifth Dimension, free from the karmic implications of the lower planes and harmonizing through the causal plane of spiritual purity and unconditional love.

Divine Plan: The intelligent arrangement and design of all situations and circumstances Co-created by the Source and the I AM Presence.

Earth Changes: A prophesied Time of Change on the Earth, including geophysical, political, and social changes alongside the opportunity for spiritual and personal transformation.

Earth Plane: The dual aspect of life on Earth.

Ehone: An angel of the Blue Flame.

Eight-Sided Cell of Perfection: An atomic cell located in the human heart. It is associated with all aspects of perfection, and contains and maintains a visceral connection with the Godhead.

Elemental: A nature-being.

El Morya: Ascended Master of the Blue Ray, associated with the development of the will.

Elohim: Creative beings of love and light that helped manifest the divine idea of our solar system. Seven Elohim (the Seven Rays) exist here. They organize and draw forward Archangels, the Four Elements, Devas, Seraphim, Cherubim, Angels, Nature Guardians, and the Elementals. The Silent Watcher—the Great Mystery—gives them direction.

Emotional Body: A subtle body of light that exists alongside the physical body. It comprises desires, emotions, and feelings.

Eshano: The Third Dimension of the Logos Web of Creation. This plane of energy is known as the "Hall of Wisdom," and is identified with active intelligence.

Everno: The second dimension of the Logos Web of Creation. This plane of energy comprises the motion of energy.

Field *(Light)*: The field of light surrounding the human body; the Aura.

Feast of Light: An Ascended Master ceremony where members of the Brotherhood meet and celebrate the light within.

Feminine: Esoteric philosophy considers the Mother Creative principle as the highest expression of being. Femininity is akin to the Goddess; it comprises one half of God whose gender is neutral. Feminine energy represents love, beauty, seduction, sensitivity, and refinement—the characteristics of the Goddess Venus. On the dark side, it reflects vanity, superficiality, fickleness, and exhaustion. Femininity is the intuition, a nurturing force which, above all, produces the first creative spark in our Sun of Truth; the female essence serves as the inspiration and aspiration for life's goodness and purity—a devotion to truth.

Fifth Dimension: A spiritual dimension of cause, associated with thoughts, visions, and aspirations. This is the dimension of the Ascended Masters and the Archetypes of Evolution, the city of Shamballa, and the templates of all Golden Cities.

Fourth Dimension: A dimension of vibration associated with telepathy, psychic ability, and the dream world. This is the dimension of the Elemental Kingdom and the development of the super-senses.

Four Pillars: The provenance of this spiritual teaching is designed to achieve the Christ Consciousness and comes from an ethereal scroll: *The Truth of Ages*. Here are its tenets, which are four fundamental spiritual teachings: (1) Turn your will over to the Universal Christ and this opens the necessary intuitive knowledge which initiates the self into Selfhood. (2) Thoughts manifest; work to transform judgments towards one another into love. (3) Remember that your spiritual path and Divine Purpose are separate and unique and attained through the ideals of Spiritual Freedom. Wholeheartedly embrace this freedom, and give it to others. (4) Love one another.

Four Pillars *(Banks)*: The dual or dark expression of the Four Pillars creates four economic powers that seek to control the Earth's material resources. In the Time of Change it is prophesied these archaic systems will falter, and the world economy destabilizes.

Freedom Star World Map: The Ascended Masters' prophesied Map of Earth Changes and fifty-one worldwide Golden City Vortices. Freedom Star's name is derived from the current *Age of Spiritual Freedom.*

Galactic Beam: A specific wave of energy that originates from the Great Central Sun. Its Rays help humanity to attain higher levels of spiritual consciousness and it adjusts the body's frequency to receive the full benefit of the Violet Flame.

Galactic Web: A large galactic grid which encircles Earth. The grid is created by the consciousness of everything throughout the galaxy including various human lifeforms, animals, plants, and minerals. The Ascended Masters often refer to any type of energy point (i.e. Chakra, lei-line, Golden City Vortex, etc.) to be included in the Galactic Web. Since the Angelic Host protects this Web of Creation, the protective web of the Angelic Host is often interchanged with the Galactic Web.

Golden Age: A peaceful time on Earth prophesied to occur after the Time of Change. It is also prophesied that during this age, human life spans are increased and sacred knowledge is revered. During this time, the societies, cultures, and the governments of Earth reflect spiritual enlightenment through worldwide cooperation, compassion, charity, and love. Ascended Master teachings often refer to the Golden Age as the Golden-Crystal Age and the Age of Grace.

Golden City Vortex: According to the prophecies, these large Vortex areas are havens of safety and spiritual growth during the Time of Change.

Gold(en) Flame: An energy field of spiritual enlightenment. The teachings of the Golden Flame are said to originate from the Pleiades.

Golden Thread Axis: Also known as the Vertical Power Current, the Golden Thread Axis physically comprises the Medullar Shushumna, a life-giving nadi physically comprising one-third of the human Kundalini system. Two vital currents intertwine around the Golden Thread Axis: the lunar Ida Current and the solar Pingala Current. According to the Master Teachers, the flow of the Golden Thread Axis begins with the I AM Presence, enters the Crown Chakra, and descends through the spinal system. It descends beyond the Base Chakra and travels to the core of the Earth. Esoteric scholars often refer to the axis as the Rod of Power, and it is symbolized by two spheres connected by an elongated rod. Ascended Master students and chelas frequently draw upon the energy of the Earth through the Golden Thread Axis for healing and renewal with meditation, visualization, and breath.

Great Central Sun: The great sun of our galaxy whose solar systems rotate. The Great Central Sun is also known as the Galactic Center, which is the origin of the Seven Rays of Light and Sound on Earth.

Great Purification: Primarily considered a Native American term, the Great Purification signals the end of one period of time for humanity and the beginning of a New Time.

Great White Brotherhood and Sisterhood (Lodge): This fraternity of ascended and unascended men and women is dedicated to the universal uplifting of humanity. Its main objective includes the preservation of the lost spirit and the teachings of the ancient religions and philosophies of the world. Its mission: to reawaken the dormant ethical and spiritual spark among the masses. In addition to fulfilling spiritual aims, the Great White Lodge has pledged to protect mankind against the systematic assaults—which inhibit self-knowledge and personal growth—on individual and group freedoms.

Greening Map: The Ascended Masters' Earth Changes and Golden City Map for Australia, Asia, and New Lemuria; this map is associated with the ecological Alchemy of the planet and the birth of the feminine in our spiritual consciousness for the New Times.

Green Ray: The Ray of Active Intelligence is associated with education, thoughtfulness, communication, organization, the intellect, science, objectivity, and discrimination. It is also adaptable, rational, healing, and awakened. The Green Ray is affiliated with the planet Mercury.

Guardian Angel: Sometimes referred to as the Christ-self, the Guardian Angel functions in tandem with the Christ-self, but works to interface various Spirit Guides and Spiritual Teachers from the Fourth Dimension, or Astral plane. The Guardian Angel is part of the Angelic Host, one of Seven Angels assigned to an individual in the physcial plane.

Heart Chakra: The location of this Chakra is in the center of the chest and is known in Sanskrit as the *Anahata*. Its main aspect is Love and Relationships; our ability to feel compassion, forgiveness, and our own feeling of Divine Purpose.

Higher Self: The *Atma* or *Atman*. This is the true identity of the soul which resides in the spiritual planes of consciousness, and although it is energetically connected to each individual in the physical plane, the Higher Self is free from the Karmas of the Earth Plane and identification with the material world.

Hilarion: Ascended Master of the Green Ray associated with the attainment of personal truth and the development of faith. Hilarion is considered to be a Master Healer and a teacher of Hermetic Law.

HU *or HUE, the*: In Tibetan dialects, the word "hue" or "hu" means breath; however, the HU is a sacred sound and when chanted or meditated upon, is said to represent the entire spectrum of the Seven Rays. Because of this, the HU powerfully invokes the presence of the Violet Flame, which is the activity of the Violet Ray and its inherent ability to transform and transmit energies to the next octave. HU is also considered an ancient name for God, and it is sung for spiritual enlightenment.

Human Energy System: The Kundalini System, consisting of Seven Chakras. The Human Energy System also contains the Divine Blueprint, a map of energy meridians and energy currents of the body.

I AM America Map: The Ascended Masters' Map of prophesied Earth Changes for the United States.

I AM: The presence of God.

I AM Presence: The individualized presence of God.

I AM THAT I AM: The Hebrew translation of this phrase into English means, "I Will Be What I Will Be." I AM is also derived from the Sanskrit Om (pronounced: A-U-M), whose three letters signify the three aspects of God as beginning, duration, and dissolution—Brahma, Vishnu, and Shiva. The AUM syllable is known as the omkara, which, as the name for God translates to mean, "I AM Existence." "Soham," is yet another mystical Sanskrit name for God, which translates into English as "It is I," or "He is I." The teachings of the I AM Activity use this translation as the meaning of "I AM." In Vedic philosophy, it is claimed that when a child cries, "Who am I?" the universe replies, "Soham—you are the same as I AM."

Interdimensional mathematics: A yet-to-be discovered set of scientific principles that explain the existence of the unseen worlds. Much of the phenomena of the New Times—namely the Golden Cities—are explained through its science.

Kellular Energy: A form of energy, toxic to the human body, created from high, but short-wave temperatures, based on the Kelvin Scale.

Kuan Yin: The Bodhisattva of Compassion and teacher of Saint Germain. She is associated with all the Rays and the principle of femininity.

Kuthumi: An Ascended Master of the Pink, Ruby, and Gold Rays. He is a gentle and patient teacher who works closely with the Nature Kingdoms.

Law of Grace: The Violet Flame is based upon this metaphysical law.

Lemuria: An ancient civilization that existed before Atlantis, largely in the South Pacific, North America, Asia, and Australia.

Light: "Love in action."

Love: "Light in action."

Logos: Wisdom.

Logos (Logoic) Web: The underlying intelligent science of creation that is woven through and connected to all created life.

Manu: Manu refers to a root race or a group of souls inhabiting a vast time period (era or epoch) on Earth. Manu is also a mythical, cosmic being who oversees the souls during their incarnation processes throughout the duration of that specific time period. Some consider Manu a type of spiritual office, not unlike a "World Teacher." For example, one evolved-cosmic being will serve as Manu for one world cycle, and when it ends, it moves on in the evolutionary process. A different entity serves as Manu for the next group. Each group of souls has a different energy and purpose. Seventh Manu children will possess advanced capabilities—astute intellect, vast spiritual knowledge, and keen psychic abilities.

Mental Plane: A field of discernable energy of the Human Aura comprising thoughts, which contain the intellect and our active intelligence.

Mother Mary: Ascended Goddess of the Feminine who was originally of the angelic evolution. She is associated with the Green Ray of Healing, Truth, and Science, and the Pink Ray of Love.

Naval Chakra: Also known as the *Solar Plexus*, this Chakra is located between the navel and the base of the sternum. It is an intense feeling (intuitive) Chakra which is known as the *Center of Power and Balance* in relationship to everything in life.

New Age: Prophesied by Utopian Francis Bacon, the New Age would herald a United Brotherhood of the Earth. This Brotherhood-Sisterhood would be built as *Solomon's Temple*, and supported by the four pillars of history, science, philosophy, and religion. These four teachings would synergize the consciousness of humanity to Universal Fellowship and Peace.

ONE: Indivisible, whole, harmonious Unity.

Oneness: A combination of two or more, which creates the whole.

Paul the Venetian: An Ascended Master of the Pink, White, and Green Rays. Paul the Venetian identifies with the qualities of cooperation and beauty through art, architecture, music, and literature.

Pink Ray: The Pink Ray is the energy of the Divine Mother and associated with the moon. It is affiliated with these qualities: loving, nurturing, hopeful, heartfelt, compassionate, considerate, communicative, intuitive, friendly, humane, tolerant, adoring.

Pleiades: A seven-star cluster that exists in the same Orion Arm of the Milky Way Galaxy near Earth. Also known as the *Seven Sisters*, the Pleiades is located in the Taurus Constellation. Its seven stars are: Sterope, Merope, Electra, Maia, Taygeta, Celaeno, and Alcyone.

Portia: Also known in Ascended Master teachings as the Goddess of Justice and Lady Opportunity. Portia serves on the Seventh Ray. She is the Divine Compliment of Master Saint Germain and her symbol is the scales of justice. As an embodiment of the energies of Divine Mother, her golden scales symbolize the perfect balance of mercy and justice. Harmony holds balance. Some say her electronic pattern, a mandala, is the Maltese Cross.

Prana or Prahna: Vital, life-sustaining energy; also known as orgone or chi.

Prahanic: The first of nine dimesnions of the Logos Web, the Web of Creation. This is a dimension of sustaining, life-giving energy.

Prophecy: A spiritual teaching given simultaneously with a warning. It's designed to change, alter, lessen, or mitigate the prophesied warning. This caveat may be literal or metaphoric; the outcomes of these events are contingent on the choices and the consciousness of those willing to apply the teachings.

Ray: A force containing a purpose, which divides its efforts into two measurable and perceptible powers: light and sound.

Saint Germain: Ascended Master of the Seventh Ray, Saint Germain is known for his work with the Violet Flame of Mercy, Transmutation, Alchemy, and Forgiveness. He is the sponsor of the Americas and the I AM America material. Many other teachers and Masters affiliated with the Great White Brotherhood assist his endeavors.

Sananda: The name used by Master Jesus in his ascended state of consciousness. Sananda means joy and bliss, and his teachings focus on revealing the savior and heavenly kingdom within.

Seven Rays: The traditional Seven Rays of Light and Sound are: the Blue Ray of Truth; the Yellow Ray of Wisdom; the Pink Ray of Love; the White Ray of Purity; the Green Ray of Healing; the Gold and Ruby Ray of Ministration; and the Violet Ray of Transmutation.

Soltec: An Ascended Master of science and technology who is affiliated with the Green Ray.

Soul Group: A family of origin, usually based upon the Science of the Seven Rays of Light and Sound. It is claimed that the origin of Earth's human race is founded upon twelve principal soul groups, known as the Council of Twelve.

Spirit: The action of the I AM or the I AM Presence on the Earth Plane.

Spirit-guide: An Ascended or unascended spiritual teacher who assists the soul on their journey of evolution and spiritual growth on Earth. A Spirit Guide resides in the spiritual planes of consciousness.

Spiritual Awakening: Conscious awareness of personal experiences and existence beyond the physical, material world. Consequently, an internalization of one's true nature and relationship to life is revealed, freeing one of the lesser self (ego) and engendering contact with the higher (Christ) self and the I AM.

Spiritual Hierarchy: A fellowship of Ascended Masters and their disciples. This group helps humanity through the mental plane with meditation, decrees, and prayer.

Star Seed: The Star Seed is a family or soul group whose members have evolved to Fifth-Dimensional awareness. Star Seeds can also contain members who have not yet evolved to this level and are still incarnating on Earth. Ascended Master teachings also refer to a Star Seed as an indication of a soul group or Ray Family of origin for which the individual possesses a natural affinity.

Third Eye Chakra: Also known as the *Ajna Chakra*, this energy center is located above and between the eyebrows. The Third Eye Chakra blends thought and feeling as perception and projection for Co-creative activity.

Throat Chakra: Located at the throat area, this Chakra is also known as *Vishuddha*. It is associated with Expression of truth, emotion, creativity, knowledge, and the sciences.

Time Compaction: An anomaly produced as we enter into the prophesied Time of Change. Our perception of time compresses; time seems to speed by. The unfolding of events accelerates, and situations are jammed into a short period of time. This experience of time will become more prevalent as we get closer to the period of cataclysmic Earth Changes.

Time of Change: The period of time currently underway. Tremendous changes in our society, cultures, and politics in tandem with individual and collective spiritual awakenings and transformations will abound. These events occur simultaneously with the possibilities of massive global warming, climatic changes, and seismic and volcanic activity—Earth Changes. The Time of Change guides the Earth to a New Time, the Golden Age.

Time of Transition: A twelve-year period when humanity experienced tremendous spiritual and intellectual growth, ushering in personal and global changes. In the year 2000, a new era, called the *Time of Testing*, got underway. It's a seven-year span of time when economies and societies encountered instability and insecurity. These years are also defined by the spiritual growth of humanity; Brotherly love and compassion play a key role in the development of the Earth's civilizations as mankind moves toward the *Age of Cooperation*.

Tube of Light: Light surges from the tributaries of the Human Energy System: Chakras, meridians, and nadis—to create a large pillar of light. Decrees, prayers, and meditation with the Tube of Light increase its force and ability to protect the individual's spiritual growth and evolution.

Unfed Flame: The Three-fold Flame of divinity that exists in the heart and becomes larger as it evolves. The three flames represent Love (pink); Wisdom (yellow); and Power (blue).

Universal Mind: The Omnipresent intelligent consciousness of the Source.

Universe: All created matter and space. Ascended Master teaching claims creation occurs at different periods of time, which results in distinctive, unique Universes.

Violet Flame: The Violet Flame is the practice of balancing Karmas of the past through Transmutation, Forgiveness, and Mercy. The result is an opening of the Spiritual Heart and the development of *bhakti*—unconditional love and compassion. It came into existence when the Lords of Venus first transmitted the Violet Flame, also known as Violet Fire, at the end of Lemuria to clear the Earth's etheric and psychic realms, and the lower physical atmosphere of negative forces and energies. This paved the way for the Atlanteans, who used it during religious ceremonies and as a visible marker of temples. The Violet Flame also induces Alchemy. Violet light emits the shortest wavelength and the highest frequency in the spectrum, so it induces a point of transition to the next octave of light.

Violet Ray: The Seventh Ray is primarily associated with Freedom and Ordered Service alongside Transmutation, Alchemy, Mercy, Compassion, and Forgiveness. It is served by the Archangel Zadkiel, the Elohim Arcturus, the Ascended Master Saint Germain, and Goddess Portia.

Vortex: A Vortex is a polarized motion body that creates its own magnetic field, aligning molecular structures with phenomenal accuracy. Vortices are often formed where lei-lines (energy meridians of the Earth) cross. They are often called power spots as the natural electromagnetic field of the Earth is immensely strong in this type of location.

Web of Creation Prayer: Saint Germain offers this prayer to recognize and bless the creative forces of Mother Earth:

I have returned. I AM peace.
I have come this day in love and goodwill to mankind.
I have returned. I AM the light. I have come this day to bond to you.
I have returned. I AM Creation, the inner spark from which you came.
I have returned. I AM.

Will: Choice.

Wisdom Ray (Yellow Ray): The Ray of the Divine Wisdom is primarily associated with the planet Jupiter and is also known as the Divine Guru. It is affiliated with expansion, optimism, joy, and spiritual enlightenment.

Appendix A
Nineteen Lessons: A Review

1. The Angelic Host. The Angelic Host links the life force of the human to the primal life force of the planet. We each have seven angels serving us, corresponding to our Chakra System. This forms a grid of consciousness known as the Galactic Web. These angels protect and guide us and are directed by our Higher Self, who cannot enter into the physical dimension. Some angels function more easily in denser areas. The Angelic Host, working within the realm of Cosmic Oneness, may appear to us with the permission of the Higher Self, to interact and to help nudge us onto our path.

Before embodiment we are given an angel of directive force known as our Guardian Angel, who is directly linked to one point on the Galactic Web. The Higher Self impresses the consciousness of the directive force angel, who then activates the other six. Through our call to our Higher Self, we become more integrated. Groups working comprehensively together share directive angelic force, which participate in split consciousness. Problems occur when these groups focus upon differences rather than similarities.

2. The Mental Plane. There are twelve specific gene pools, or families from the Council of Twelve, upon the Earth. These are all part of the ONE true family of Spirit. Found within the collective pool is the mental realm. The mental plane, the mind, has been given for us to collectively understand the element of Spirit, the activity of the I AM. We developed this mental plane but we must now learn to let it go to allow the entry of the collective, universal Spirit. The mental plane can create blockages which keep us away from pure Spirit. The mind can create a thought form with a life of its own, without Spirit.

We have come into the Earth Plane with the function of raising the body. This is done through a series of events, or lessons to move through, to gain in collective consciousness and become of greater service to others. We have the choice to stay after a series of experiences or to transition to other realms of consciousness to receive enlightenment. There is a great benefit to being in human form during this time of great growth and learning, attunement – collective reviewing. There are some who have been brought to interfere, to tempt, and to test. Yet, all things work together as ONE in classroom Earth.

The Earth Changes are a reflection of mass consciousness. It is up to us to attain eternal freedom. There is no place for fear while humanity integrates the Christ Spirit. When the heart is totally integrated with the I AM Presence, we are enfolded within the loving, nurturing hands of our Parents. The healing of the Earth is assured and our healing comes from knowing what is true as we come to a point of unity. Physical dis-ease, or not being at ease with the path we have chosen, is a separation from Source and does not allow Source to work with us. This help is always a part of us and due to us, as we are conductors of this great energy Source. The lesson is to trust what is given and how we choose to see.

3. Free Motion. The Earth is also awakening to her destiny to serve as a great light; a place where people as entities of like force, come to move through and walk with the Energy Vibration of Emotion. The soul's growth and greatest gain has always come through the vibration called emotion. The greatest force to awaken the cellular memory is allowing e-motion to move through our light bodies. The emotion moving is neither good nor bad and is jostling the cells as the Christ Spirit is speaking to the self, "Awake and join me. Awake and become ONE with me." Light harmonics, those colors associated with Cellular Awakening and memory, move within the cell, flowing emotion through the spiritual body, giving it life and light and preparing it for Co-creation. Cobalt Blue and Gold assist this freedom of motion through the spiritual body and can break up congestion of the spiritual self, where one encounters much within their physiology and much within their mental capability which allows disintegration of the physical vehicle.

The purpose is to integrate all for free movement, free flowing, free motion, e-motion in and out of all that is contained within universal knowledge and principle. To grasp this and move with it will produce a flow into free motion. The DNA relates to the Godhead and cellular memory, stating strongly I AM THAT I AM. The Awakening Point or Eighth Triad integrates the Chakra System into ONE and is a point of reference, calling from itself to join with the Source, to join with those of like harmonic vibration and to join the awakening Earth Planet.

4. Rapture and Ascension. It is the sincere heart that steps forward to do this work. It is the sincere heart that truly believes in itself. To initiate the Ascension process, it is necessary to balance ourselves and bring forth the momentum of internal peace which can be extended to the external world of chaos. Peace comes to one through internal being, acceptance, joy, and laughter. Peace is the state of moving through the human emotion and finding within the mental states and through the mental states, the point of being to accept the self. Four Rays of Love raise the vibration through Cellular Awakening: Green, the ministration of self for self healing; Pink, the ministration of self for self love; Violet, transformation within the self, to bring forth directed purpose; and Gold, the synthesis of being, an acceptance of self in service. It is the service that we extend to others that raises vibration and as we extend ourselves to others, we also receive.

The Ascended Masters will assist all who ask. See the light within and hold it close, bringing it forth and nurturing it as you would a child within the womb. Know that you are Beloved and cherished. Healing energy flows from the end of the index finger; the primary vibration comes forth, forming a web of energy and an electronic substance throughout the ends of the fingertips. This comes forth from the universal supply.

Rapture means the acceptance of Ascension. Astral travel does not achieve this. Astral travel is the ability to use the mental mind/body to move within the light-field. Ascension uses all bodies. You can walk into the next dimension through the command, "I AM THAT I AM." It is a command from the Word, the Source, the Logos, the Creative Force. It is forceful enough for you to make your Ascension on this scientific formula alone. Combine this with the Violet Flame for Purity, Forgiveness, Mercy, Compassion, and Transformation. Use laughter to look at the self. This removes the sense of judgment of the self.

5. The Extended Will. Through our approval, the Ascended Masters may radiate energy to us to enhance our connection to our I AM Presence. Turning our will over to our Source is the extended will, which is cared for and nurtured by members of the Spirit or Tribal Family. The individualized will is that which seeks to become an individualized, creative energy source.

The use of raw foods is recommended, entering into higher light activity, for not only are they flushing, they are nourishing to the Solar Plexus Chakra. Master Teachers recommend foodstuff that is vacuum-packed and in powered-form for longer term storage. All that we need is present in universal substance but as the increased energies radiate to the planet, we will have less need for food energy and will be drawing upon the universal Prahna. Developing and working upon the Universal Mind merges all to ONE Mind. Carry the message of love, for the message of love is the thread that weaves us all together. Extend love to everyone, not only to those within our groups, and share this message.

6. The Web of Creation. There are nine specific regions which cover the Earth Plane and Planet and bring forth the Vortex energy points, containing nine layers or dimensions. The Earth, divided into quadrants, is woven with a golden course of light, moving between and around the quadrants. This is part of the cloth that is woven between this planet and the Solar System and it assists us to become aware of the essence of our energy, the source of our energy, and the mass consciousness of the planet. Our vibrations can help to attract our Brothers and Sisters of the Galaxy and draw an interaction of their vibrations toward us. These energy points are like logistic locations of a nervous system and by which way we project a thought and our physical presence, we are able to make contact through these points of sensitivity, points of access. The body contains union. We live in a world of willing whole Spirit, committed to all.

7. Cellular Instruction. With Time Compaction, time is accelerated and we feel a quickening. Fourth Dimensional consciousness is that which no longer requires the density of the Third Dimension and an acceleration of the cells of the body comes to reunite us to our mighty I AM Presence.

The planet itself is a structure most closely associated with the cellular level of mankind and since man's body is made of Earth, it contains the same genetic coding and Cellular Awakening. All is accelerated for the urgent call for healing. There is healing that is occurring at the physical level but also at other levels, as all physical ailment is a manifestation of that which has occurred at the finer levels within the etheric code. Within the etheric body, there are many levels and fine adjustments to be done. The finer bodies are an expression of Spirit. Spirit threads the light-bodies together and weaves them together as ONE. There is no separation between each of the bodies; however, there is a distinguished individuality of each, so we are able to utilize the energies of each for our use.

Channeling requires the conscious use of the will to raise one's vibration. All those who are willing are called. Dietary adjustments assist this preparation, such as the elimination of all animal products, as well as the use of the Violet Flame. When entering into sleep, call to the Higher Self to allow your channel to open. This will lead the body at night to go up to a place of instruction for opening to the higher energies. Use the Golden Ray to improve the quality of the food ingested. Extend this Ray from the left hand through the ring finger, which is specifically in alignment with that of the Golden Ray, and visualize a band of gold light coming through the food. You will notice less desire for the use of animal products. Also recommended is water mixed with fruit juices, fruits that come specifically from the Golden Ray. This fruit has a skin or flesh of a golden color, especially bananas or citrus fruits; also, no more than one-tenth vegetable product or protein.

Passion is associated with Spirit and passion is associated with the fire element. Fire within the mental capability utilizes prayer, affirmation, and the will of God. This passion is a direct link of Spirit, the mighty I AM Presence, to that of the Heart Chakra.

8. The Personality. The work of healing resonates from the planet out to the cosmos, touching not only our lives but those who will unlock another Solar System. To understand healing, it is necessary to understand the personality, which is a collective force of many, many embodiments. The personality is not real; it is only the result of a healing force working in our lives. The personality is the reactive force. As Spirit descends into the physical realm, it takes a healing path to remove the many splinters within its nature of being. There is weeping and inflammation as this process occurs. Yet, the weeping and the inflammation that we see is temporary. The personality serves a purpose and should be thanked and acknowledged for the gift that it gives, for it allows the skin to become strengthened and better able to resist the penetration by another splinter.

There are those living upon the planet who have embodied with a compulsive, addictive nature. But this has been a spiritual gift to clear and to cleanse much within the soul. Many have chosen this path for its quick and fast results. A person who asks for assistance is a person who recognizes a need to have more clarity and to become stronger. This great collective force in the universe has stepped forth to cloak our bodies with a teacher. This great teacher, the personality, has come to give us much. Be thankful for trials and tribulations, for we are loved for our purpose. Life is the energy force of the ONE, whose nature is to flow. Our Spirit is strengthened with the universal principles of Forgiveness, Compassion, Grace, and Love, for these are the Divine Attributes of the soul.

9. Collective Cooperation. The work of the heart, the love energy, is the common thread, the common goal, and the total resonance of this planet. Those who come to embody on Earth have come to learn to feel this energy in its highest vibration. Fourth Dimension is the functioning Heart Chakra where all become ONE. We all start as ONE and differentiate in our embodiments, working through the physicalness of our nature and the mental capabilities. Then, we rise to the point of the Fourth Dimension, the love vibration, closely associated with the Cellular Awakening. We are to learn to feel the ONE commonality, the ONE vibration which merges each energy vibration to the next. And that is love.

Feeling disharmony, we are able to sense a state of separation. And through this state of separation, we experience discomfort. Through discomfort, we can be moved to hopelessness or helplessness. This, too, is a point of Cellular Awakening, for we are driven and directed. Our cells spin in such a way that there is no other way for them to go and we surrender to love. A time of great need is a Time of Awakening and a time of a monumental leap and rejoicing. The focus of Earth Change information is for people to unite and to see themselves as ONE with Divine

Purpose, ONE as a cooperative unit, and ONE who must work together to seek active solutions to the problems we have.

Only those who are able to work cooperatively, collectively, and in harmony will be staying through the great changes. We will be able to see and know a person by their work. We are brought to this planet to restructure and to live in joy. All barriers and walls will be broken down as we start to understand the love vibration which beats within all hearts. We will give freely of ourselves to our Sisters and Brothers and our Sisters and Brothers will give freely back. The work is self-conscious correction, to exercise our truths, and work together in a cooperative way to synergistically live these truths.

10. Emergence. The Violet Flame is the highest principle to use during this Time of Transition. This transformation is called through the Higher Self to the universal Source for the Flame of Mercy and Forgiveness. This can be extended to others, as well as to ourselves. It can be called through the affirmation: I AM A BEING OF VIOLET FIRE. I AM THE PURITY GOD DESIRES. Or, through the visualization of the Violet Flame, starting at the base of the feet, coming up and surrounding the body, enveloping it in an egg-like shape. The Violet Flame is then encircled with the white pure light, known as the Tube of Light. Around this Tube of Light, call upon the Blue Flame for protection and to ever sustain truth.

The Earth Changes are a force that we work with, but not a force which stays constant, and it changes in a Co-creative way each day. The upcoming Earth Changes have been preordained through the collective consciousness of mankind for two thousand years. And so, there are changes which are inevitable, which must come, such as the removal of separation; the movement from Third to Fourth Dimension consciousness; and the healing of the human body, transfiguration. Ascension is the process of rising up into ONE with the Higher Self. This happens through the many layers of the mental, emotional, and etheric or astral layers. The direct approach is to call to our mighty I AM Presence and to ask for the Cellular Awakening.

The timing of one dimension merging with the next opens dimensional gates and we are able to perceive and partake of all dimensions at once. It is a period of time known as Transition. We can listen for sounds which allow the human body, through the Chakra Centers, to align to harmony. There are tones which assist the Cellular Awakening, as well as the use of color and its vibration, the use of light and different densities of light, and the use of prayer and affirmation. Sound aligns one to the many universes which are in existence and universes of other dimensions within the Earth Plane and Planet. Harmonization of cosmic energies entering in at this time integrates with color and light for the Cellular Awakening.

There is an anti-Christ, a entity who is acting with a collective force, which serves its part in our awakening. These collective energies, as they are placed in our path, are there to test us and for us to learn the art of discernment.

11. Seven Bodies. As our consciousness shifts from Third to Fourth Dimension realities, the body de-densifies, taking on its new shell and the electromagnetic currents of the other bodies must be aligned. There are seven layers within the physical body, each corresponding to the energy points known as Chakras. Each must be aligned with the electromagnetic current of the planet, also having seven layers, starting from the core and extending to the outer surface. And beyond this, there are again seven layers outside of the Earth surface, known as the higher body of the Earth. We are created like the Earth, a combination of two sparks, the Mother and Father Principle, that of the Earth substance, our physical shell, and the Logos, or Spirit. Spirit comprises the higher realms, the spark of Divine Creation; and the Mother Principle comprises the fertile ground which the Spirit has been planted upon.

With total integration and completion, we are ready for transfiguration or Ascension into the alignment area of the Fourth Dimension. This is a reality of harmony and cooperation, where we learn to control the energies of the seven lower bodies and seven higher bodies, to create with them and attain At-ONE-Ment. This prepares us for Fifth Dimension reality, that which is the combined collective force of both layers, where one is able to move in and about through density and through Spirit at will.

The lower bodies begin with the Mother Principle, the fertile ground of nurturing, where the Spirit is planted. This is the will to create, the creative energy ready to be impregnated with the Divine Spark of Creation. The two work simultaneously together. The next body is the will to survive, the survival instinct, the deep desire and need for life to continue and also the need to nourish and to protect. The next body holds the need to move to community, to work together as ONE, not through the love principle but the urge to be ONE with our Source. This is the need for like organisms to move together. The move to community is closely associated with the development of the lower mental body. In higher Divine Principles, it is the structure and orderliness of Creation.

The next body relates to the development of the emotions. Through the emotional body, life forms evolve and move from genetic memory to Cellular Awakening. This body is linked to the Heart Chakra and the point of impregnation from the Father Spirit, which is spiritually anchored within. This is the Source of the Spirit, the center from which it comes. The next body extends the emotional body to others of like-mind, those who have developed their emotional body as communication through the Throat Chakra.

Next is the Third Eye Chakra and we are developing this as we move from Third to Fourth Dimension. This develops beyond the mental capability and the Mother Principle to collectively and constructively work with the other Chakras. This Chakra must be developed to allow telepathic communication with other Star Systems. This Chakra works as a sensing organism for harmony and cooperation among the masses and is sensitive to the collective force, the mass consciousness. Its development relies heavily on the surrounding collective consciousness within a 240 kilometer radius. This is why there is the deep need for a person to live in a certain, specific area.

Then, we move to an emerging point on the body known as the "Gate." This point opens and closes like a gate between the Mother and Father Principle. Once mastered and understood, we can travel between these two worlds. This movement is not a matter of development; it is a matter of natural cause. There is nothing that will stop this. It is just so. There are times that this development is delayed but a delay is only an interval in time.

The Earth follows the pattern of the mass consciousness. The sixth body is known as the collective body. Our bodies have been formed of the Earth substance and with the actions through Spirit, form the collective consciousness of the Earth. The ability to read the Earth and feel the Earth occur through the Cellular Awakening, as the cells become ONE with the Mother Principle. The Father Principle verbalizes and takes a course of action with the right use of will, utilizing the gift of freewill. This also activates the awareness of the Prahna, the universal substance from which we draw energy. In a similar fashion, the Earth too draws the collective force of other Solar Systems and planets. We are being prepared to move Home, as the Prodigal Son, and we are welcomed with a gladdened heart. It is not a matter of giving up the physical; it is a matter of mastering the physical to understand, honor, and nourish the Mother Principle.

At this point, a quickening occurs and we enter into Divine Service, extending to others what is within us. This is the work of integration of the Mother and Father, a time to rejoice, for we have been called Home.

12. Sound Technology and Sound Teachings. The Cellular Awakening occurs not only on an individual basis but on a collective basis. That is a reason to move into a community or group, for as we move within these groups, we obtain a quickening, which is known as the collective Cellular Awakening. This is based upon the universal idea, "Where two or more are gathered in the name" and the Hermetic principle, "as above, so below." The seven points upon the human body correspond to seven points upon the Earth Planet, as the Rays of Divine Guidance, Divine Truth, Divine Wisdom, Divine Love, Divine Abundance and Prosperity, and Divine Transformation. As these centers open, they integrate. The properties of electromagnetism and color, also understood as high frequency sound, correspond to one another and serve one another. This is a healing process.

Each Chakra corresponds with a specific sound and color vibration: "A" corresponds with the First Chakra, most associated with red and brown; "E' is associated with the Second Chakra and the yellow vibration; "I" is associated with the Third Chakra and green; the Fourth Chakra, the heart, with "U," or "HUE," which is closely associated with two color-sound vibrations, green and pink; the Throat Chakra corresponds to the blue intensity, also surrounded with golden light; the Third Eye Chakra mixes purple with yellow; and the Crown Chakra merges all colors into what is known as white Christic light. It is the Crown Chakra which also combines all these sounds into one common sound.

The principle of the Mother, comprising the body upon Earth, generates electromagnetic currents to allow light to enter into the system and sound vibration to resonate within. As she has brought herself forth to offer her assistance for our planetary embodiment, her lower frequencies use the higher properties of stone and water to bring forth total integration of the Chakra Centers. The lower density sound vibrations work with the cleansing of elements within the life stream of the body. The higher frequencies deal with the spiritual self, the spiritual body. The body and Spirit contain complementary properties, where the universal laws and principles, "as above, so below," apply equally to the construction of the human body. Physiology reflects the spiritual essence and our work is to integrate these two.

The desire of the soul to serve utilizes the highest vibration and motivation. Technologies can accelerate this desire of service, even though prayer provides a simpler path. Technologies can assist those who need to release energy and remove energy blockages. Blockages occur not only through previous embodiments but through the movement from genetic memory to Cellular Awakening.

Within the Principles of Grace, it is important that we work with joy in our hearts and nurture our work. Enjoying Co-creation will keep us from pushing or driving ourselves. Service diminishes separation and opens gateways and portals. The physical body, expressing the eternal light body of the spiritual essence, becomes a receptor. At night, we use our true, inner body to bring forth the information received through the receptors during the day. We sense, not only our planet but that of other Galaxies, Solar Systems, and Planetary Systems and may also travel to these. The true spiritual body, the Higher Self, remains intact as a spiritual force and travels to sense and to bring back information to us in the physical.

Most of the animals work with sound vibration. We carry within our auric field, a sound vibration that harmonizes or blends with the sound vibration of a particular species. Some animals adjust their frequencies quite readily and communicate through this sound resonance. It is important to understand our sound and to feel, harmonize, and blend this with more species. We can increase our comfort through investigating other sounds. The pitch of our voice is also the pitch of our auric field. Communication does not come through the brain, which only serves as a relay. True communication comes through the Higher Self, to be opened by the individual we intend to reach.

Our body is not real. As spiritual beings, our body and Earth have been given to us to express our Spirit. When we see the bodies around us, not as bodies, but as Spirit, we will know that we live and walk and breathe in the world of Spirit.

13. From the Golden Beam. As we are spiritually readied to move into a new reality of multi-dimensional consciousness, it is of vast importance that we reconnect with our Source, so we may function as a full God Being. Cataclysmic Earth Changes may occur if we do not realize our spiritual path of life and the spiritual way of being. All is Spirit and as we move through matter, we must honor and respect this in all that we do, all that we see, and all that we are. This is the current challenge facing mankind, those who have forgotten the vastness of the Source. The physical body has been given to us as a great gift. It is a joy to be able to be ONE with Spirit and ONE with the Elemental natures. It is a joy to take a walk within a forest and to touch and to smell and to breathe the air. This is a matter of rapture within the moment, recognizing the other aspects of what we are. There is a deeper intrinsic meaning in all that we are. All is Spirit and as we move through this collective way of being, we will reconnect to Source and express this Source in all our activities.

The mind functions, not in Spirit and not in the physical. Yet, the mind can torture us with thoughts, penetrate the flesh, and penetrate the Spirit. We have come now, to release the mind and to give ourselves to Spirit. Divine Wisdom is wisdom which is known as Divine Order. The constant, steady thoughts and the tinkering within this realm of being have the tendency to encase us in fear and bring those fears forth into reality. The point is to be who we *really* are.

14. Feminine Principle. The Feminine Principle is associated with feeling, intuition, and the lower chakras of the body, which hold the point of conception and the womb of nurturing. We have been brought to this planet to understand not only our many aspects and our interaction with the aspects of others but to understand the principles of the feminine planet. The Earth is brought forth as a nurturing place and has been referred to as the Garden. Throughout the ages, there have been many Times of Transition when the fruit is ready and the Garden is harvested.

When bought to this point of the harvest, we need to choose what is appropriate for our individualized path. Perfection is attainable at many levels, the perfection of the physical body and of the material illusion. Illusions are brought to us so we can understand how the material world is illusive. Through understanding illusion, we are brought to the point of Mastery of the material. As we move in the field of material illusion, we must recognize all things as temporary and all things as instantaneous. It would be impossible to embody upon the physical plane without the effect of the collective thought form. We have come here to experience this, which is a point in time, as we call history, or an era or epoch. We choose a point of reference to experience the collective form.

Thought is most powerful: if we linger upon joy, we become joyous. Mankind has perceived thought as negative and positive but both are dynamically parallel, so we may experience many things and choose where we would prefer to be. The mind has been given to us as a great tool, so we will choose to use the heart. Yet, a heart that does not use the mind, gives with free abandon and its energy is wasted and dissipated. The heart that gives through the choice of Divine Intelligence, opens to the clear use of giving.

15. Alignment. Do not take the Beloved Flame within the heart and throw it to those who do not understand. Rather, gather it up and bring it forth in Divine Service, the extension of our self to another. This is achieved through choosing the Vibration of Love. Each day, we consciously make the choice to love each other and each day, we must consciously make the choice to love ourselves. The Violet Flame of Mercy and Forgiveness contains the Law of Grace. When another comes with words to instill fear in us, this golden Law of Mercy and Forgiveness is brought to set us free.

As the Spirit, or I AM Presence, fills and penetrates the body, the body searches to become aligned to particular geophysical areas to enhance its being. We have been given a mind that discerns and a body that walks upon this planet but the heart is the fine way of being. Brought here as a Divine Creation and an extension of the world of Spirit, it is most important during this Time of Planetary Transition to enjoy the life of Spirit. There is a fine balance that occurs between physical matter and the Spirit, for the physical body is the densification of Spirit. As we give to this alignment, we are ready to receive. There are areas of the Earth to travel to for alignment, alignment not only with that of the Earth itself but that which reaches through the cosmos to other planetary systems. Each one carries a mission within their fine blueprint, for as Divine Inheritors, we have come here to be, to learn, and above all, to serve.

Prayer and meditation are of vast importance and when visiting a geophysical for alignment and spiritual growth, find a spot to sit and become still. Then visualize a golden beam of light coming from the Higher Self through the Crown Chakra and running down the spine. Become familiar with the Earth at this location, for molecular structures are in alignment with other planets. Each location, every square foot, is a mathematical calculation. As the Higher Self integrates with the physical, we begin to understand the Cellular Awakening and through this Cellular Awakening, we move through various lands to experience specific locations.

As the energies of the Higher Self flow, the alignment process removes blockages. Sensing the planet as a living organism, we can feel that the body is made of Earth through the Mother Principle. As we travel to specific locations, we can feel the Father and Mother integrating as ONE. Where they merge, we can align ourselves.

We need the comfort of feeling our Presence surrounding us at all times. When we encounter those with differing auric fields, it is especially important to call to the Higher Self to bring a Tube of Light into our energy field and surround it with the Blue Flame. The Blue Flame comes from the Angelic Host, ministering directly with the Elemental Life Force. This is the time for us to be who we are and to let no one interfere with that. We can call for strength to be who we are and allow others to be who they are.

16. Transformation. The use of the Pink Ray of Divine Love and Compassion is greatly needed during these Times of Change. When the Pink Ray integrates with the Blue Ray of Divine Will and Truth, this combination forms the transformation upon the Earth Plane and Planet. The planet, resonating with Divine Intelligence, acts and reacts to our actions and reactions. So, it is most important that we learn through our mental states, the difference between action and reaction, to bring ourselves to the state of inner peace.

The Energy Vortices of the planet, outlined in the map of upcoming Earth Changes, are places we may go to purify our body and become ONE with the Source. The vortex areas are the locations where this Divine Consciousness is allowed to flow in a more direct stream, as a more pure form of her collective state. These vortices are sensory organs of the Earth, where she perceives as we do through our Chakra Centers and sensory organs. During this time of cleansing and purification, the healing of the organism and collective consciousness of the Earth occurs, as well as the healing of our bodies. The physical body will soon no longer be needed for expression. We are Divine Inheritors, not only of this Garden from which we sprang but Divine Inheritors of eternal wisdom, love, and power. It is important to focus upon the use and acknowledgement of the I AM Presence, guiding and directing us with our freewill as a Co-creative force.

Our bodies are changing in direct alignment and correspondence to the collective consciousness of the planet. We are in the process of Ascension. This is a day-at-a-time progression. Ascension is not a process that occurs over night but is a continual spiritual practice. Demand, "I AM a Divine Inheritor, I AM a Child of the Garden, I AM come that I AM THAT I AM." This awakens our cells and the right use of will as a Co-creative force and the I AM Presence becomes the focus within our lives.

As we call forth the perfection of the cells within our bodies, Auras, or energy fields around our being, we can say: "I AM the Violet Flame, I AM Mercy, I AM Forgiveness, I AM Divine Compassion, I AM the Violet Flame, I AM Perfection, I AM ONE with Peace, I AM the Violet Flame, I AM Transformed, I AM THAT I AM." This eternal transmuting flame comes forth and grants forgiveness of the past, forgiveness of the future, and places us in the timeless present. This is the Cellular Awakening.

17. Relationships. Remember that what we see in another, we have in ourselves. In the relationship between children and their parents or sponsor, each serves as a mirror for the other. There is a spiritual contract that is signed between the sponsor and the child for the guidance and nurturing of this child up to eighteen years of age. The first nine years, the child is liable under contract and the parent and child implement this contract to its fullest extreme. The second nine years, the child is allowed more freedom within the contract.

We may select a mate who is a clear mirror of ourselves or who merely stands side by side, in a reciprocal relationship. Since we are experiencing Time Compaction, many karmic relationships from the past need closure. Yet, simultaneously, all relationships are ongoing and eternal. Relationships are founded on one principle, love, a choice that we make for peace through our actions. Making a choice for peace, we act in a loving way and our relationships never end when we act in such a manner. They are in a continuum of the process of externalizing our internal peace.

Those forces that guide and direct us, speaking within our heart, are available at all times for us to call upon, to open those doors and pathways to create happiness and joy in our lives and in all that we do. We are perfect and whole as we are and can rejoice as ONE with the Source. To gain the clear understanding of the Source is to walk our individualized path. It is up to us to understand the use of the will, the use of love, the use of wisdom, and the use of power.

We have been created by the Source, in the image of this Source, to experience the gifts of this Source. The path through human embodiment is to experience the individualized Presence of God. To learn such a quality entails interacting with the qualities of others, for what is love without loving one another and what is love without wisdom.

18. Transitional Events. It is most important to eliminate struggle and strife from our lives and find the path of least resistance. This is also the path of enlightenment. The country grows with its needs for government but the true needs and the true wants are for spiritual freedom and spiritual power. One clearly cannot come from a source of inner strength without being empowered by Spirit. We each possess the Christ Consciousness, ready to emerge and come into full bloom through the Cellular Awakening. There is much strife and struggle in our governments. Our prayers, light, and love can help at this Time of Change.

To love the self and heal the body, see the body as an extension of the lovely Spirit within. The body has been brought forth to express this Divine Spirit that we truly are. Each cell within our being is a densified form of our spiritual self. We are guided, loved, and wanted and we have a role to fulfill on the Earth at this important time. It is no accident that we are here.

Our companion animals have been brought forth to soothe us. We gain and learn many spiritual lessons from our precious animal friends. Animals function through a collective consciousness, which they tap into, and because of their devotional service to humanity, they will be offered the Divine Spark.

The Spiritual Masters ask for a halt in the use of animal products in our diet. Those animals which are domesticated for our planet, particularly the cow, have a developed emotional body and field. We are being asked to not take their emotions upon ourselves. Fish have not absorbed emotional qualities quite so densely and is an easier form to take into our system; however, we are being asked to no longer take animal products of any kind, including eggs and milk. We are being asked to become ONE with our Divine Plan and Blueprint to assist in our Cellular Awakening.

At the cosmic levels, our cries for peace brought about Time Compaction. It is being ushered in through, not only the wind element, but that of the fire element. The wind element carries the cosmic rays to our being. Advances are made much more quickly through Time Compaction, making great leaps possible.

There has been much control of information about the plan and purpose of the Hierarchy on the Earth Plane and Planet. Information has been kept hidden from the general public of specific events and dates that are literally written in stone. It is most important that this information be made public, as having this information could avert the creation of fear in the hearts of mankind. Keeping vital information secret is the ego functioning at its fullest. We are being asked to call forth Divine Wisdom, the Light of God that Never Fails, and the Violet Flame, not only for ourselves but for those who are intentionally withholding the keys to unlock these secrets.

19. In the Image and Likeness. The collective energy force called I AM THAT I AM is at our beck and call. When we call on I AM, there is a direct alignment of the energy force. When we call this into motion and choose to love, it is the right use of our will and action, action being power. We are God beings who have been put upon this planet to be responsible for our energy and to balance our love, wisdom, and power. Emotion allows the world to come forth. There are particles within emotion that serve the right use of will, the e-motion in balance and harmony. The emotional body is part of our energetic and genetic make-up, being made in the image and likeness of God.

It is a discipline and a great work to stay in the middle of the emotional pendulum. This pendulum functions within the circle of eternal Creation and remaining within this circular motion, one comes to the point of the spiral, allowing one to ascend in motion. Through the use of the Decree of the Violet Flame, the Law of Mercy and Forgiveness, one's energetic bodies will remain within the spiral motion. This Violet Flame spiral holds an electromagnetic trail of those who have gone before, their energies left graciously for us to pull upon. As we reach the energy of an Ascended Master and merge, we collect attributes from that energy and then become separate again.

In the New Times, gold will be freely circulated for its use as a vibration. If we are concerned about our economy and our exchange of money, we are to look at the exchange of our personal energies, as that will determine the flow of our resources and our contribution to the economy. The Earth Changes bring a great cleansing and the joy of Fourth Dimensional reality. The Great Ones of Light are coming, to be embodied upon the planet during a period of one thousand years.

Our individual origins are the Great Central Sun and we exist within the final universe created, the Christos Universe. Our Fourth Dimension is an alignment area, where the physical and the spiritual meet and merge as ONE. Total alignment of all nine Chakras occurs here, allowing us to come into full manifestation.

This book ends with this signature piece: I will take my leave from you now and offer you the Cup as you gather. Remember who I AM and, above all, never forget who you are. Bless you one and all, I AM.

Index

W

About Lori Toye

Lori Toye is not a Prophet of doom and gloom. The fact that she became a Prophet at all is highly unlikely. Reared in a small Idaho farming community as a member of the conservative Missouri Synod Lutheran church, Lori had never heard of meditation, spiritual development, reincarnation, channeling, or clairvoyant sight.

Her unusual spiritual journey began in Washington State, when, as advertising manager of a weekly newspaper, she answered a request to pick up an ad for a local health food store. As she entered, a woman at the counter pointed a finger at her and said, "You have work to do for Master Saint Germain!"

The next several years were filled with spiritual enlightenment that introduced Lori, then only twenty-two years old, to the most exceptional and inspirational information she had ever encountered. Lori became a student of Ascended Master teachings.

Awakened one night by the luminous figure of Saint Germain at the foot of her bed, her work had begun. Later in the same year, an image of a map appeared in her dream. Four teachers clad in white robes were present, pointing out Earth Changes that would shape the future United States.

Five years later, faced with the stress of a painful divorce and rebuilding her life as a single mother, Lori attended spiritual meditation classes. While there, she shared her experience, and encouraged by friends, she began to explore the dream through daily meditation. The four Beings appeared again, and expressed a willingness to share the information. Over a six-month period, they gave over eighty sessions of material, including detailed information that would later become the I AM America Map.

Clearly she had to produce the map. The only means to finance it was to sell her house. She put her home up for sale, and in a depressed market, it sold the first day at full asking price.

She produced the map in 1989, rolled copies of them on her kitchen table, and sold them through word-of-mouth. She then launched a lecture tour of the Northwest and California. Hers was the first Earth Changes Map published, and many others have followed, but the rest is history.

From the tabloids to the *New York Times*, *The Washington Post*, television interviews in the U.S., London, and Europe, Lori's Mission was to honor the material she had received. The material is not hers, she stresses. It belongs to the Masters, and their loving, healing approach is disseminated through the I AM America Publishing Company operated by her husband and spiritual partner, Lenard Toye. Working together they organized free classes of the teachings and their instructional pursuits led them to form the School of the Four Pillars which includes holistic and energy healing techniques. In 1995 and 1996 they sponsored the first Prophecy Conferences in Philadelphia and Phoenix, Arizona.

Other publications include three additional Prophecy maps, four books, a video, and more than sixty audio tapes based on sessions with Master Teacher Saint Germain and other Ascended Masters.

Spiritual in nature, I AM America is not a church, religion, sect, or cult. There is no interest or intent in amassing followers or engaging in any activity other than what Lori and Lenard can do on their own to publicize the materials they have been entrusted with.

They have also been directed to build the first Golden City community. A very positive aspect of the vision is that all the maps include areas called, "Golden Cities." These places hold a high spiritual energy, and are where sustainable communities are to be built using solar energy alongside classical feng shui engineering and infrastructure. The first community, Wenima Village, is currently being planned for development.

Concerned that some might misinterpret the Maps' messages as doom and gloom and miss the metaphor for personal change, or not consider the spiritual teachings attached to the maps, Lori emphasizes that the Masters stressed that this was a Prophecy of choice. Prophecy allows for choice in making informed decisions and promotes the opportunity for cooperation and harmony. Lenard and Lori's vision for I AM America is to share the Ascended Masters' prophecies as spiritual warnings to heal and renew our lives.

Books and Maps by Lori Toye

Books:

NEW WORLD ATLAS SERIES
Volume One: I AM America
Volume Two: The Greening Map
Volume Three: The Map of Exchanges

FREEDOM STAR: *Prophecies that Heal Earth*

GOLDEN CITY SERIES
Book One: Points of Perception
Book Two: Light of Awakening
Book Three: Divine Destiny
Book Four: Sacred Energies of the Golden Cities

I AM AMERICA TRILOGY
Book One: A Teacher Appears
Book Two: Sisters of the Flame
Book Three: Fields of Light

Maps:

I AM America Map
Freedom Star World Map
United States 6-Map Scenario
United States Golden City Map

I AM AMERICA PUBLISHING & DISTRIBUTING
P.O. Box 2511, Payson, Arizona, 85547, USA. (480) 744-6188

For More Information:
www.iamamerica.com
www.loritoye.com

I AM America Online Bookstore:
http://iamamericabookstore.iaabooks.com

 About I AM America

I AM America is an educational and publishing foundation dedicated to disseminating the Ascended Masters' message of Earth Changes Prophecy and Spiritual Teachings for self-development. Our office is run by the husband and wife team of Lenard and Lori Toye who hand-roll maps, package, and mail information and products with a small staff. Our first publication was the I AM America Map, which was published in September 1989. Since then we have published three more Prophecy maps, nine books, and numerous recordings based on the channeled sessions with the Spiritual Teachers.

We are not a church, a religion, a sect, or cult and are not interested in amassing followers or members. Nor do we have any affiliation with a church, religion, political group, or government of any kind. We are not a college or university, research facility, or a mystery school. El Morya told us that the best way to see ourselves is as, "Cosmic Beings, having a human experience."

In 1994, we asked Saint Germain, "How do you see our work at I AM America?" and he answered, "I AM America is to be a clearinghouse for the new humanity." Grabbing a dictionary, we quickly learned that the term "clearinghouse" refers to "an organization or unit within an organization that functions as a central agency for collecting, organizing, storing, and disseminating documents, usually within a specific academic discipline or field." So inarguably, we are this too. But in uncomplicated terms, we publish and share spiritually transformational information because at I AM America there is no doubt that, "A Change of Heart can Change the World."

With Violet Flame Blessings,
Lori & Lenard Toye

For more information or to visit our online bookstore, go to:
www.iamamerica.com
www.loritoye.com

To receive a catalog by mail, please write to:
I AM America
P.O. Box 2511
Payson, AZ 85547

CPSIA information can be obtained
at www.ICGtesting.com
Printed in the USA
BVHW051745250123
657139BV00024B/544